"HONEY, ARE YOU LISTENING?"

Dr. Rick Fowler & Jerilyn Fowler

A
JANET
THOMA
BOOK

THOMAS NELSON PUBLISHERS
Nashville • Atlanta • London • Vancouver

Published in Nashville, Tennessee, by Thomas Nelson, Inc., Publishers, and distributed in Canada by Word Communications, Ltd., Richmond, British Columbia.

Unless otherwise noted, the Bible version used in this publication is THE NEW KING JAMES VERSION. Copyright © 1979, 1980, 1982, 1990, Thomas Nelson, Inc., Publishers.

Scripture quotations marked NIV are taken from the HOLY BIBLE, NEW INTERNATIONAL VERSION.® Copyright © 1973, 1978, 1984 by International Bible Society. Used by permission of Zondervan Publishing House. All rights reserved.

Library of Congress Cataloging-in-Publication Data

Fowler, Richard A., 1948–
    "Honey, are you listening?" : how Attention Deficit Disorder could be affecting your marriage / Rick Fowler, Jerilyn Fowler.
        p.   cm.
    ISBN 0-8407-7710-8
    1. Attention-deficit disorder in adults—Popular works.
    2. Attention-deficit disordered adults—Family relationships.
    3. Communication in marriage.   I. Fowler, Jerilyn.   II. Title.
    RC394.A85F68   1995
    616.85′89—dc20   94–40543
                                                                  CIP

Printed in the United States of America.
4 5 6 — 00 99 98 97 96 95

"Honey, Are You Listening?"

Other Books in the Minirth Meier New Life Clinic Series

The Anger Workbook
Dr. Les Carter, Dr. Frank
Minirth

Don't Let Jerks
Get the Best of You
Dr. Paul Meier

The Father Book
Dr. Frank Minirth, Dr. Brian
Newman, Dr. Paul Warren

The Headache Book
Dr. Frank Minirth

Hope for the Perfectionist
Dr. David Stoop

Imperative People
Dr. Les Carter

Kids Who Carry Our Pain
Dr. Robert Hemfelt, Dr. Paul
Warren

The Lies We Believe
Dr. Chris Thurman

Love Hunger:
Recovery from Food Addiction
Dr. Frank Minirth, Dr. Paul
Meier, Dr. Robert Hemfelt,
Dr. Sharon Sneed

The Love Hunger Action Plan
Dr. Sharon Sneed

The Love Hunger
Weight-Loss Workbook
Dr. Frank Minirth, Dr. Paul
Meier, Dr. Robert Hemfelt,
Dr. Sharon Sneed

Love Is a Choice
Dr. Robert Hemfelt, Dr. Frank
Minirth, Dr. Paul Meier

Love Is a Choice Workbook
Dr. Robert Hemfelt, Dr. Frank
Minirth, Dr. Paul Meier

Passages of Marriage Series
New Love
Realistic Love
Steadfast Love
Renewing Love
Transcendent Love
Dr. Frank & Mary Alice
Minirth, Drs. Brian & Deborah
Newman, Dr. Robert & Susan
Hemfelt

Passages of Marriage
Study Guide Series
New Love
Realistic Love
Steadfast Love
Renewing Love
Transcendent Love
Dr. Frank & Mary Alice
Minirth, Drs. Brian & Deborah
Newman, Dr. Robert & Susan
Hemfelt

The Thin Disguise
Pam Vredevelt, Dr. Deborah
Newman, Harry Beverly,
Dr. Frank Minirth

Things that Go Bump in the Night
Dr. Paul Warren, Dr. Frank
Minirth

The Truths We Must Believe
Dr. Chris Thurman

For general information about Minirth Meier New Life Clinic branch offices, counseling services, educational resources, and hospital programs, call toll-free 1–800-NEW-LIFE.

To our son, Chip (and to his future wife . . . whomever that may be), who brought our unspoken struggle to the forefront and helped us understand ourselves.

Contents

Acknowledgments

*To Sandy Dengler, who helped us
in organizing and expressing our
thoughts. Her creativity and insights
are greatly appreciated.*

ADDmitting the Problem

J eri speaks:
When I married Rick, I promised my dad I would never divorce. But I don't think I made any promises about murder, and right now, that looked like a viable option. On the other hand, since we were moving—that was the circumstance igniting this particular bad situation—maybe I could just go without him and refuse to send him the new keys. Whatever, I *had* to do something. Rick was driving me right out of my tree.

"Rick!" My voice rang about a hundred decibels too loud. "What are you doing now?!"

"Packing the stuff from the broom closet." He grinned winsomely. "Look! The mop exactly fits in this corner of the wardrobe carton, and if you put the broom in at a slant it fits too. Now you don't have to—"

"But we still need all that stuff! We have to clean after the furniture's out. That stuff's the *last* to go!"

He looked like a kid with forbidden chocolate smeared all over his face.

As furious as I was, I felt guilty, too. He was so proud of his coup; it was a clever packing job, and I had just rained all over his party.

You know how opposites attract? Rick and I took that to extreme. At moving time, I planned how to tackle the job and then methodically packed nonessentials first, essentials last. Rick, like a grain combine, went through the house scooping everything up willy-nilly and spitting it out into whatever box he passed. It didn't matter if the box contained stuff from the kitchen *and* a bedroom *and* the spare room *and* the living room. He gave the job absolutely no thought.

Heaven knows I tried to be patient. I explained over and over, "All right, look. I pack only kitchen items in this carton marked 'kitchen.' Then in the new house, I set this carton down in the kitchen and unpack it and put everything away. One room. Boom boom, it's done. That way, I don't have to run all over the house putting something here and something else there. Kitchen stuff in the kitchen box." I struggled to keep the irritable edge out of my voice.

But he instantly bristled with resentment, and why shouldn't he? By the time our numerous discussions about logical ways of packing had ended, I was taking my anger out on whatever I was packing at the moment, and he was flinging out sarcasm thick enough to float a brick.

It's true, moving is stressful under the best of circumstances. But our lives went on like that all the time, moving or not, stress or not. As much as I loved Rick, I was at my wit's end. Someone was going to have to change, and it wasn't going to be me. After all, I was right and he wasn't.

I was the one who used my head.

Rick speaks:

I love moving! Different surroundings, new experiences, fresh beginnings. I enjoy challenges, like making fragile round objects fit safely in square cardboard cartons. I like shifting furniture around in the new room, experimenting with looks and concepts. If you're disorganized, why sweat it? You'll find everything eventually.

But Jeri did her level best to quench the fun. She couldn't just move. She had to move in a thoroughly organized manner. No matter what I did, it wasn't what she wanted done that moment. Mostly to keep me out from underfoot, she'd assign me tasks. I'd get started on them, get bored, see something else that needed doing just as much, and divide my efforts. I didn't see anything wrong with that; it all had to be done sooner or later.

Before I married Jeri, I was used to constant criticism. I'd been getting it my whole life. Being used to it, though, isn't the same as liking it, especially when it comes from your spouse. Her unjustified frustration with me (well, *I* thought it was unjustified) would really torque me off. Then I'd dump on her; we're talking heavy verbal abuse here. There were times I hurt her deeply. What should have been a happy relationship was rapidly dissolving into constant pain and acrimony.

BRILLIANCE UNAPPRECIATED

When Jeri married me, little did she realize that I share much in common with Albert Einstein. For instance, my guidance counselor told me, "Don't even bother to think about college. You'll never make it." When Einstein's father asked young Albert's headmaster what profession his son should prepare for, the headmaster ostensibly replied, "It doesn't matter. He'll never make a success of anything."

The man who made sense of the cosmos kept forgetting his key. He'd have to awaken his landlady to be let in. He never knew how much money he made. Even as he left those details of finance to his wife, the world's greatest physicists and mathematicians were flocking to his advanced courses to get a taste of his brilliance.

Jeri relates, "Rick? Yeah, he forgets his key every now and

then. *But* when the only engine of the airplane he was flying threw a rod at 1,500 feet, he knew exactly what to do. Calmly and casually, he set the plane down in an open field with no harm to anyone."

Albert Einstein and Rick Fowler and Sir Winston Churchill and Jay Leno and an unbelievable number of others now and throughout history all display a series of characteristics we have labelled Attention Deficit Disorder. Call it by its acronym, ADD.

ADD has been recognized in children for some time now. At first those in the medical profession glibly assumed the condition just sort of went away as a person grew up and his nervous system matured, and for many people it does to some extent. Now, however, psychologists and physicians are beginning to realize that not only does ADD often persist through adulthood, it is the cause of immeasurable heartache in many adult lives.

Human relationships at every level—parent to child, husband to wife, brother to sister, friend to friend—all suffer, not because someone is wrong but because someone is intrinsically *different*. Made differently. Wired differently. And that is the saddest suffering of all, for there is no wrong to point to, no blame to lay. Certainly, lots of so-called wrong is cited and plenty of blame flares back and forth, but it's all misplaced.

It seems that very often an ADD adult will somehow choose a non-ADD logic freak for a partner and soul mate. In many ways the ADD mate and non-ADD spouse complement each other. Unfortunately, too often they each find the other's differences irritating, especially as time unfolds and the relationship matures. Married persons tend to polarize. That is, instead of becoming more like each other, the two partners often take extreme positions as if balancing an invisible teeter-totter. One becomes more responsible as the other grows more reckless; one becomes more solemn as the other grows more carefree. They both spend their entire life together trying to fix the faulty partner.

The most difficult relationship an ADD adult can attempt is to team up with a perfectionist. Picture an accountant who must reconcile books to the penny working with an accountant whose motto is, "If it comes out within five bucks, it's balanced." In my marriage counseling I have seen many divorces result from this attempted wedding of the perfectionist and the ADD adult. My experience suggests that perhaps twenty percent of *all* marriage problems stem from ADD tendencies in one of the spouses.

Married over twenty-six years, we have learned by trial and error (lots of trials and plenty of error!) to forge a relationship that works past the problems. Ours is not a happy-ever-after story; it is a we're-hanging-in-there story that gets easier and better as time goes by. We have each accepted the changes we must make individually in order to create a successful marriage that by all rights should have failed, and it succeeds well.

The ADD person must make significant changes. So must the spouse. The non-ADD spouse must go the extra mile to tactfully help the ADD mate compensate for his or her differences. The ADD mate also has a long mile to walk, making changes, adjusting to the realities of the majority world. Is the effort worth it? Absolutely! Is it impossible for some people— that is, have some couples drifted past the point at which repair is possible? We don't think so.

We want to guide the person with Attention Deficit Disorder and the spouse as well toward a more compatible relationship. We know this: If each person goes along as that person is predisposed, disaster generally follows. Crushed spirits, broken marriages, and lifetimes of heartbreak will extend beyond the affected couple into their children, their friends, and their relatives.

If a man and woman who both have ADD marry, just as much pain is likely to result. It will appear to arise from other causes, but the root cause—ADD—will be the same. Those couples will probably suffer financial problems, which always place a strain on marriage. They will probably find opportunities slipping by and frustrations with life mounting. They often blame each other. Each of them yearns for a mate to take over the onerous, routine duties of life, and both will be denied that.

How about you? The fact that you're reading this book suggests that you believe ADD might be a factor in the problems you or people close to you face. If it is, we have good news. Not only can you get around the problems wrought by ADD, you can make the condition work for you to enrich, advance, and beautify your life.

That's quite a claim. Are we overstating it? Not in the least. The adjustments require both hard work and a spirit of cooperation on the part of both mates. Once those adjustments begin to show fruit, you'll never want life any other way—and certainly not the *old* way!

Trust us on that.

Understand that dealing with ADD, or suspected ADD, is no cure-all. It is misdiagnosed, under-diagnosed, over-diagnosed, ignored, and given too much attention. Although a formal diagnosis carefully made is an immense step forward, the first thing you have to do is assess signs and symptoms rather than worry too much about diagnosis.

IDENTIFYING THE SITUATION

A lot of people claim Attention Deficit Disorder is messing them up when that's not the situation at all. Much blame gets laid on ADD that ADD doesn't merit. It is frequently diagnosed where it doesn't exist, and not infrequently its presence is missed altogether.

Only a competent counselor can clearly and correctly identify real ADD. If you feel it is a factor in your life or in the life of a person you care about, professional assessment is necessary. The initial step, however, is to become informed so that you can become an active participant in the therapy process. So let's look at the situation from two perspectives: first, let's see what ADD is and what it does. Then let's use a fun sort of questionnaire (those of you with test anxiety, relax; you'll enjoy this one) to see how ADD or an ADD-like condition might be marring your happiness and marital peace.

Right Brain Versus Left Brain

Your brain is built in symmetrical halves. It doesn't show up well in pictures, but it's actually two separate parts, one on the left and one on the right, so closely pressed together that it looks like one round organ. The two halves are connected by a short, tough cable. All the data flowing between the two halves passes through that cable, the *corpus callosum*. (The cerebellum, a pair of hemispheres of its own, connects its two parts with its own separate cable.)

The two halves of your brain do different things; they specialize, you might say. The right half handles the bulk of creative thought and brainstorming. It works with the abstract, the intuitive, the immediate. It views life and problems more or less globally, looking at the whole picture all at once. The left half deals with logic, math, language, straight-line sequential thinking. To the left brain, one and one are invariably two. To the right brain, one and one could, under the right circumstances, be eleven.

Do you remember the dance between a square and a triangle on *Sesame Street?* The stodgy old square could get bigger or smaller, but it remained ever and always a square. And it was proud of its stability and steadfastness. Squares are quite useful. They measure land and other surface areas. As alphabet blocks or buildings, they serve people well. They are constant. In contrast to the square, the triangle danced all over, changing from an isosceles triangle to a scalene triangle to an equilateral triangle to a right triangle, stretching, bending, flexing, singing. The triangle teased the square for staying always the same, and the square extolled the virtues of stability. The square was quintessentially left-brain, you see, and the triangle was right-brain.

Lefties love routine and order. Righties abhor it. Lefties prefer sameness. Behaviorally, they are conservative. Righties are the opposite.

In most people, data flows freely between the two hemispheres, balancing tastes and skills. In some people, however, one hemisphere may predominate. Those people exhibit the strengths of one side but not the other.

Left brainers are amazingly well organized. They think in linear ways, arrange data in mental files easily accessed, and appreciate detailed organization. They do very, very well on examinations and working with computers because they think the way that tests and computers are designed. Binary. Black and white. Straight-line logic. Left brainers tend not to trust intuition.

Right brainers may know an inordinate amount of information, but their brains cannot access the information quickly and easily. It's in there somewhere; getting to it is the trick. They do poorly on tests even though they may know as much or more than the left brainers who score higher. Their brains pick and grab from a wide world of sensations and information. They are *global* in their approach to their surroundings rather than linear. (Lefties would call it scattershot.) For right brainers, logic is secondary to intuition. They tend not to sweat details. They appreciate impulse and spur-of-the-moment much more than lefties do. They need not plan elaborately. The hard core among them do not bother to plan at all.

Needless to say, left brainers do not appreciate right brainers, and righties think lefties waste a lot of time in detail and criticism.

"They're like early birds and night owls," a friend explained, smiling. "The night owls love to stay up late and sleep in the next morning. The early birds turn into a pumpkin at nine and are up before the sun. They don't appreciate each other. They almost always marry each other, ever notice? *However,* the owls are content to let the early birds go flittering off at the crack of dawn. If forced into wakefulness, the owls stuff up the crack and go back to sleep. Live and let live. You don't see owls proselytizing early birds. But those early birds are constantly trying to convert the owls! Trying to get owls to think it's neat to get up with the sun."

That's a great analogy because that's how righties and lefties function. The righties don't try to force lefties into the right-brain mold. But the lefties are constantly trying to get the righties to "Quit being lazy," "Just apply yourself," "Be more like us (correct) people," "Don't be so scatterbrained," "Get organized." Nag, nag, nag.

The Right-Brained ADD Mate

In most cases, people with Attention Deficit Disorder are extremely right-brained. (There are other factors also in true-blue ADD people, which we'll discuss, such as the presence and quantity of neurotransmitters.) That's one of the reasons that ADD individuals often clash with the majority of the rest of the population. Lefties fit comfortably into our modern world. They maintain schedules and order. They fit seamlessly into the educational system because over these many years the system has been fine-tuned to accommodate and encourage the kind of thinking that happens in the left hemisphere of the brain.

If you're a teacher, it's a lot easier to write a bunch of dates up on the board and watch your pupil soak them up than to have to work some kind of hands-on mnemonic to shove those dates into the pupil's memory. Teachers enjoy students who can take on facts and figures like a car takes on fuel at the gas pump and then show off on tests—because that kind of student makes their job easy.

But not many students are left-brained enough to absorb information that way. Those who are form the high-performance end of every school's grading bell curve. Guess who fills in the other end, the failing end.

What's a bell curve? A bell curve is a statistical graph shaped pretty much like the Liberty Bell. It has a big hump in the middle, denoting the majority of scores or whatever, with a tail stringing out to the left and another to the right. When the bell curve is a graph of students' grades, the area to the right indicates the number of students receiving A's and high B's, the area to the left indicates the low D's and F's, and the C's, low B's, and high D's form the vast middle. Few schools *officially* assign grades using a bell curve, but too often teachers consciously or unconsciously try to make the grades they give fit that shape. A teacher or professor can't give everyone an A without appearing too lenient in grading. On the other hand, if all the grades are too low, the educator seems unfair or too difficult or unskilled as a teacher. The bell curve sends the unspoken message that the teacher's grading system, perfectly fair and just, reflects the pupils' learning capacity.

All too often, what a bell curve really reflects is the fact that about 20 percent of people are strong lefties, another 20 percent are strong righties, and the majority of students exhibit the strengths of both brain hemispheres. Most of the time, grades have little to do with native intelligence at all.

Complicating the picture is hyperactivity, the inability to sit still and focus attention. A lot of ADD kids—a majority of them—are also hyperactive. They're a handful in traditional classrooms, especially when large class size is a factor. Teachers can't keep a lid on them, can't keep them interested in the work.

Now add that hyperactivity to the inability to blot up information the way lefties do, and you see why ADD individuals reach adulthood with serious problems. They often cannot show academic proficiency, the measure by which jobs and respect are awarded. They may still have hyperactive tendencies, making them difficult to cope with in the eyes of many coworkers. And in part because they've been bouncing off the walls, at odds with the "real" world, they lack social skills.

Carry all that into a marriage and you have trouble with a capital *T.*

Assessing Your Tendencies

Jeri is comfortably left-brained. You don't outgrow that. I'm intensely right-brained. You don't outgrow that, either. When I was a kid, ADD was not yet recognized. However, I have from childhood displayed the symptoms of ADD. Some people grow out of ADD, ending up with activity levels and brain function in the broad normal range. But a surprising number of people do not. They carry their inability to concentrate well, and often their high activity and impulsivity level continue to thrive through adulthood. I am one of those people.

Whether or not you have actually been diagnosed with ADD doesn't matter much if you display the tendencies. Signs and symptoms are the important things, because the behavioral tendencies associated with ADD are what do a marriage in. They are what the non-ADD mate must deal with. So let's explore in the form of a quiz whether these ADD tendencies might be giving you trouble in your relationships. Mark your gut-level reaction to these situations.

Are ADD Tendencies Giving You Trouble?

A word of explanation here: From now on, I will be using the word *you* to mean either you or a person you care about.

1. You are about to move to another house or apartment. The first thing you feel like doing is:
   A. making a list.
   B. scrounging some boxes out of the garage.

2. You are talking to a casual acquaintance about a subject very dear to your heart. The other person expresses disagreement with your position.
   A. You listen carefully, gauging exactly where the viewpoints differ, and decide whether it's worth it to argue.
   B. Immediately you mount a convincing defense of your position.

3. It's Saturday. You have to change the spark plug in the lawn mower, mow the lawn, put out the curbside recycling bins, and write some letters.
   A. You install the plug, mow the lawn, rest, put out the bins, and write the letters during the evening when it's cooler and you can sit outside.

B. You put out the metal-recycling bin, start a letter, find the spark plug, finish the letter, install the plug, mow part of the lawn, remember you didn't put out the glass and newspaper bins, do that, watch a TV sports program as you start another letter, finish the back half of the lawn, drain the car crankcase, mow the side lawn, put new oil in the car, start a third letter because you're stalled on the second one, check the timing in the car, vacuum the car's interior, and vow to finish the lawn tomorrow because it's too dark to see.

4. You and your mate are discussing the problems of a person in your church and how the church can help that person. The next day you talk about it with your pastor:
   A. The two of you offer the pastor some suggestions.
   B. Both of you protest, "But that's not what I said yesterday!" discovering a basic lack of communication.

5. You are watching the TV game show *Jeopardy.*
   A. Unless you choked under pressure and went blank momentarily, you'd probably do pretty well as a contestant.
   B. Bunch of egghead show-offs from another planet; that's what they are.

6. You are clearly the victim of injustice.
   A. You do a slow burn and plot either revenge or justice.
   B. You blow sky high and try to work immediate retribution.

7. As a child you were diagnosed, correctly or incorrectly, as being hyperactive or having ADD.
   A. Not True.
   B. True.

The *B* answers, as you've guessed, are the red flags. If you could truthfully answer them, "Umm, sort of, I guess," or if you waffled between options, you're not what we might call a foaming-at-the-mouth rightbrainer. If you want to explore this prospect further, try the longer, more formal quiz we've included as Appendix C. It will give you a clearer idea about the extent of possible ADD problems.

If you feel strongly that the guy responding with *B* to most of the items in this quiz is your kind of person, or that the extended quiz in Appendix C describes you or your mate all too well, your ADD signs and symptoms may well be causing problems in your relationships.

BEATING THE ADD PROBLEM

We have been struggling with this bag of problems for years. Our son Chip is an ADD kid. I counsel many individuals with ADD difficulties as part of my practice with the Minirth Meier New Life Clinics. So we've been around and around the block when it comes to ADD in adults. We are confident the answers and discussions offered in these chapters will help you get past the barriers to fulfillment and joy that ADD or an ADD-like condition erect. We will talk about the basics of marriage— communication, money handling, intimacy, affection, friendship, and compatibility.

ADD affects all of those components and more. But it need not scuttle your ship of dreams. Jeri definitely wants to stress that the ADD mate brings significant advantages to a relationship. We'll assist you in tapping into them.

It will help to remember that the ADD mate is like anyone else only more so. That person needs more reassurance, more patience, more encouragement, and more direction than do most people.

You'll see what I mean as we discuss the first and probably most important aspect of a marriage, communication. You think you know about good communication? The ADD mate will make it a whole new ball game.

TWO

ADDressing Others: Communication

Jeri speaks:
I'd ask Rick to do something and he'd do maybe half of it. For instance, I'd ask him to clean up the table after dinner. He'd take the dishes to the sink, but that was it. The butter was still out, the place mats hadn't been put away—the job was half done. If I told him I wasn't satisfied with the job, he said I was nagging. Most of the time I ended up finishing the job myself, irritated and fuming silently or, more often, sighing loudly enough to be heard in the next room. If Rick asked what was wrong, I would usually respond with a martyr's look and say, "Nothing. I'm just tired and I still have *so much to do*." I guess I knew that I wasn't playing fair, but I was sure that if I didn't let him know he was wrong, it would just promote greater carelessness the next time.

And the things he'd say! Whatever popped into his head flew right out his mouth. He wasn't sensitive to other people's feelings at all. Mine in particular, it seemed. I'd think, "That jerk!

How can he say he loves me when he'd let *that* slip out?" And then I'd curl up in a little hole and smile and pretend it was all okay.

Rick speaks:

I remember once we were going to do a lot of Saturday morning running around. You know—go here, go there, get all these things done. Hey, that's my kind of day! Jeri had her list, of course, and the word *Payless* was written at the top.

We piled into the car and away I went to Payless Lumber, eager to prowl those aisles. Jeri gave me this icy stare. "Rick, I meant Payless Shoes."

It seemed like so much of our communication went that way. I'd hear something and form an idea of its meaning in my mind. So did Jeri. Well after the fact, we'd discover that neither of us had formed the same idea. We were talking. We were explaining things to each other. But we sure weren't communicating.

WHAT ADD ADULTS BRING TO COMMUNICATION

We ADD folk are actually pretty good at communication, but like Frank Sinatra, we have to do it our way. There are several elements of the ADD adult's personality that encourage good communication.

THE ABILITY TO SHARE FEELINGS EASILY

Sharing feelings is very hard for a lot of people. Yet if you stuff your feelings, you block communication. Jeri did that a lot in the beginning. In her desire to prevent friction, she let me go my merry way without telling me how my words and actions really affected her. She had to learn to open up, to make herself vulnerable. The ADD mate is not going to pick up messages about feelings—or anything else—spontaneously.

You've often heard that one of the big problems in many marriages is that each spouse assumes the other can read minds. You hear things like, "Well, if he really loved me, he'd know I don't like such-and-so." "I so want her to do this-and-that! Why won't she?!" It takes a while for some people to realize that mental telepathy ("I want a sports car for my birthday. I want a sports car for my birthday!") gets them nowhere.

The ADD adult isn't going to bother sending out any telepathic messages, but pretty quickly you will know how that person feels about something. About *anything*. Jeri claims I hang it all out like wash on a line.

Sometimes the gift for expressing feelings backfires when it is matched with the ADD adult's natural impulsivity. Often feelings are shared instantly with whomever is handy.

Happy? Tell the world! That's okay unless you're at a funeral. Angry? Dump it on whomever is handy. Unfortunately, you can burn a lot of innocent people that way. The ADD adult goes away feeling fine. He got it off his chest. But the dumped-upon victim is often hurt and furious.

The non-ADD mate can help out a lot here. He or she can deal with this Jekyll-and-Hyde aspect of expressing feelings in a couple of helpful ways.

Let the ADD mate know that he or she is speaking inappropriately.

We don't recognize what's inappropriate, but we want to know. Arrange a signal. It can be a kick in the shins, a loud "Harumph," or a couple of tugs on the ear. Whatever. Work something out. This will save both the spouse and the ADD mate potential embarrassment and problems.

Of course, the other side of this coin is that the ADD mate has to decide in advance to accept the spouse's judgment call as being accurate. It's really easy to brush off the spouse's subtle or not so subtle signals.

Don't assume mind reading.

Open up. It took Jeri ten years to realize she had to change in this respect, and she still struggles with it at times. She still wants to back off from confrontation or friction, even though she knows absolutely that it's neither wise nor healthy to do so.

Remind your ADD mate to stop and think.

Let's face it. We ADD adults all too frequently blurt out our thoughts and feelings. We need our spouse's good ear and common sense at times we least think about it. We're not going to remember, "Think before you speak" when we're all wrapped up in a conversation, even though we very much wish we could. We're just not wired that way. Our spouse can perform a real service by hauling in the checkrein.

With their stark honesty tempered by their spouses' good sense, ADD adults contribute to good communication in another important way.

Naturally Outgoing and Talkative

Ever get stuck at the dinner table with someone who answers all your questions with "yep" and "nope"? Try keeping up an interesting conversation; you can't because it takes two to tango. ADD adults often provide good radio or TV interviews for this reason. Get them started on a subject and they'll talk. Nothing frustrates an interviewer quicker than to ask a question and get a monosyllabic response and then dead air.

ADD-like adults can get people talking and keep the conversation flowing. It takes a good talker to make good communication happen, in other words, and the ADD mate qualifies in spades. We're not just catalysts, either. There's another way we contribute to good communication: perception—at times.

Perceptive—If We're Interested

Even though I'm not good at discerning signals in casual conversation, when I'm working as a counselor and therapist, I pick up on tiny details. Counseling is my passion, my interest, you see. When I'm working, I'm *working*. An ADD friend of mine whose interest is motocross can talk for hours about bikes and competition. Talk to him about any other subject and he bounces around like water on a hot griddle.

ADD folk are just as good at thinking in depth as anyone else when it comes to their field of interest. Winston Churchill, an ADD adult, did one thing well. Actually, he did several things well; I'm referring, however, to his conduct of the British defense during World War II. He devoted his full attention to the prosecution of Britain's interest and success, and he did it probably better than anyone else could have.

We bring that same focus to conversation. And we contribute by providing lightness and fun.

Humor

ADD adults seem to have a special touch for goofy humor. Sometimes our joking gets a little raw, even hurtful. We don't, as a rule, have a lot of finesse. Right-brain humor, I guess you'd call it. Left brainers are dry and polite. Not off the wall. (Frankly, I know a couple left-brain friends who wouldn't get the point of a joke if you stuck 'em in the eye with it. Left brain and humor don't always go very well together.)

Hyperactive kids often clown a lot. This is where that broad humor gets started, I suspect. It's an attention getter. It brings a certain identity. They might not be good academically, and they might be driving the adults around them nuts, but they can save the day by bringing a smile. The kids learn early to clown around because they're naturally good at it, and they carry the habit into adulthood.

It may seem that we're suggesting that ADD adults have a leg up on communication. Not really. We have some strengths, but there are several ways in which we shoot ourselves in the foot, too.

What in an ADD Adult Hinders Communication?

On the Fast Track

ADD individuals tend to think a sentence or two ahead of what they are saying. The brain gets ahead of the mouth, so the mouth quits before a sentence is finished and starts the next sentence, trying to keep up. Our handwriting is usually poor for much the same reason. We think faster than our hand can form the letters.

After years of marriage, non-ADD mates can sometimes understand us even when we fail to complete the thought. But we must never ever assume our mate already has that skill! If the thought is incomplete, the non-ADD mate ought to call a halt and ask the spouse to rephrase, repeat, recast the thought. The idea is to communicate. Half a loaf may be better than none, but half a thought is a thought not communicated.

Sarcasm

You should expect it, actually. Because we let feelings surface, anger floats right to the top. Mix an irreverent sense of humor with a short fuse, and you've got sarcasm.

Now Jeri is pretty good with it, too. Most people can be. But she doesn't let it fly in all directions. And unless the ground rules for using it and reacting to it are well in place ahead of time, sarcasm can really damage a relationship. It belittles the person being scalded. It gouges at that person's sense of self-worth. It creates fun by causing pain, and that sort of nonsense should have gone out of fashion with the gladiator's games in the Roman colosseum.

Down at the very deepest level, sarcasm is an expression of control and insecurity. If by my acid tongue I can control your feelings and run you down, especially in public, I'm in charge of the situation, and control is a big, big issue with ADD adults. We'll get it any way we can, and a caustic wit is one of the tools that comes easiest for us.

For the longest time, Jeri let my sarcasm, both intentional and unintentional, hurt her. She suffered in silence to the detriment of us both. Now she knows better. There are two ways in which the non-ADD mate can be of real help.

Don't let snide comments go unchallenged.

Refusing to let such comments slide is really hard to do. Jeri has learned she must say something like, "I feel as though you're trying to hurt my feelings by [making fun of my comment], [joking at my expense], [belittling me], [fill in the blank]. I won't accept that."

But what if the ADD adult makes a sarcastic snip in public? The ADD mate made the comment in the presence of others; rejecting the ploy in the presence of others is not out of line. So go ahead and challenge the remark just as if you were having a private discussion. Making the ADD adult uncomfortable about the unseemly remark may be the medicine to cure the problem.

In any case, don't carry a grudge. That's lethal to any relationship, especially a marriage.

Be forgiving.

Forgiveness should be extended by both partners, of course, but it will be especially difficult for the offended loved one. Jeri has had to forgive me a million times over. And I have forgiven her. It's an ongoing process, not a once-and-done thing.

There can be much to be forgiven, for above all, we ADD adults are, to quote the old saw, bulls in china shops conversationally.

A Lack of Finesse

No surprise there. I'm just mentioning it to remind you that an ADD adult's social ineptitude can crop up anytime. Lack of finesse can sometimes sabotage a conversation. The non-ADD spouse must constantly remember that what comes out of the ADD spouse's mouth has not been sifted through the filter of sensitivity that most speakers employ.

I can only quote the famous love chapter in 1 Corinthians. To paraphrase, "Love is not touchy. Love remembers the best and forgives the rest" (13:4–5). Look on our lack of finesse as lapses in gentleness but never see them as lapses in love.

Another way in which we can hinder communication is that we are pretty hard to follow sometimes.

Scattered Thinking

Although we can often focus intensely on a particular subject, most of the time our thoughts fly like buckshot from a sawed-off shotgun. And the farther from our interest the target is, the broader the pattern. Our minds are often bounding off in three or four directions at once.

That's not all bad. When you're communicating at a surface level, especially with several people, the way you would at a party or some other informal gathering, keeping the topics flowing is an asset. Scattershot thoughts don't damage communication when the level of communication is not intense or deep.

But at home, when the non-ADD mate is trying to get an in-depth discussion going on a topic of limited interest to the ADD spouse (upcoming dental appointments, the leak in the back porch roof, or the elder child's desire to own a hamster), that scattering of thoughts can be maddening.

How can the non-ADD mate combat it? Bring the conversation back to the subject, over and over if necessary, until the salient points are worked out. Usually, the more scattered a mate's thoughts, the more focused the other mate's thoughts are. Spouses tend to polarize that way. So the ADD mate must allow the non-ADD spouse to control the conversation until the necessary talking has been completed.

Finally, ADD adults hinder conversation by failing to tune in well to the other speaker.

Nonverbal Clues

Missing nonverbal clues wouldn't be such a handicap if it weren't true that up to 70 percent of normal communication is essentially nonverbal. That's body language, facial expressions, tone of voice, and sounds other than words. For example, how would you interpret:

someone wagging her head and saying, "Tsk tsk"
someone standing in front of you with her hands on her hips, glaring
someone talking a mile a minute and wildly waving his arms
someone hunched over, hair partly covering his eyes, staring at the floor
someone with crossed arms and a tapping foot, staring at you

If that last someone is a police officer, you're in big trouble. Even the most obtuse ADD adult would try to interpret the signals if the uniform suggested potential problems. In casual circumstances, though, we would probably miss the intent of many of the nonverbal signals above. What most people would instantly read as anger, reprimand, joy, or enthusiasm and all often slides right past us. This is one of many reasons ADD adults and hyperactive ADD children are in hot water so much. They don't read the signals and don't realize it's prudent to back off.

Again, I point out: it all depends upon your area of special interest. Take the self-conscious person (hunched over, looking at the floor) above. A lot of teens come into my office with exactly that hangdog look. I can spot troubled kids quickly, just by their body language. I've learned to read body language as a part of my job. But it's strictly a job-related skill. At home, Jeri has to abandon subtle cues in favor of hitting me over the head with a frying pan. (I'm speaking figuratively, thank goodness.) I understand that, similarly, police officers will remember detailed interrogations of suspects, but on the way home they can't remember to pick up bread at the store.

How does the non-ADD mate deal with this lack of discernment? By being obvious and forceful. When a frown or a clearing of the throat might not get the word across, an outright "Quit tapping your pencil, please," does the trick.

There is one area of married life where unspoken cues are essential—sexual communication. Ah, the subtleties of flirtation! The sigh, the soft caress, the casual touch. Nearly all such romance is lost on the ADD mate.

Sexual Communication

Elizabeth Barrett Browning wrote in her *Sonnets from the Portuguese,* "How do I love thee? Let me count the ways." The poem is a paean to sensitivity and beauty. The ADD mate can probably count the ways he loves on one hand—and have a finger or two left over.

This lack of sensitivity is frustrating to the non-ADD mate to say the least. She tries to flirt with her spouse, and nothing happens. Or he may orchestrate the romantic moment the way all those magazine articles and marriage enrichment books suggest, and nothing happens. She touches her ADD mate affectionately, and he actually recoils. Talk about a turnoff! His wife is so distracted by TV that he's considering lying across the top of the set with a rose in his teeth, but he knows it wouldn't do any good. She'd go cut herself a piece of pie before she'd get the idea.

Intimacy, not just sexual intercourse but true closeness between man and wife, requires focus. You know the old saying about two lovers gazing into each other's eyes by candlelight? Intimacy requires that kind of intense focus. He and she and nothing else in the world. An ADD adult has a terrible time mustering up that kind of concentration. Too many distractions easily break it.

Frequently, ADD adults are unusually sensitive to casual

touch, and not in a positive way. Thus they recoil from what was intended as a loving gesture.

The non-ADD mate will be the first to notice the damaging lack of intimacy in a relationship. The non-ADD mate is therefore the logical person to initiate steps to improve intimacy and reverse the deterioration of the marriage relationship. I suggest four specific actions to start with. Develop other steps for increased closeness as your particular marital circumstances dictate.

Call Attention to the Problem

No carefully phrased innuendo. No vain expectation of some mysterious romantic realization. Set your mate down and explain graphically what you think is missing and what you want to do to improve things. Note I said what you *think* is missing. Don't talk to your spouse with an attitude that says, "You poor romantically-impaired jerk"; instead, your attitude should say, "I feel we need improvement here." See the difference? Not accusing. Not judgmental. Please! Not patronizing but helpful and hopeful.

Set Aside a Date Night

You can't believe what a tonic a night out without the kids can be. For one thing, it says as nothing else can, "I'm committed to *you.*" It's also a blessed relief for both spouses to get away a while. Most important, it helps your ADD spouse focus clearly on what he or she is supposed to be focusing upon: you. The distractions of chores, the phone, the kids, the television set all fall away. Non-ADD couples can possibly get by with sporadic date nights. An ADD mate needs date night once a week at least.

Don't Let Feelings Mess Up Romance

This one's a biggie in ADD/non-ADD relationships.

As I in my obtuse way gallop through life, I too often leave Jeri in the dust, frustrated and disheartened and trying to brush herself off. She might be offended by something I said or did, or she might be discouraged by something I failed to do. And it's a two-way street. I get really angry sometimes over things that I should never be upset about.

The anger and hurt and irritations happen in any marriage, but they seem to come with particular frequency to an ADD-affected marriage. That's probably because ADD people are on such a strangely different wavelength from non-ADD mates. Therefore, it's especially important for an ADD-influenced marriage to leave hurt and anger at the bedroom door.

"No, I'm sorry," said a friend of ours, the non-ADD spouse of a hyperactive man. I mean *hyperactive*. He's always doing two or three things at once, and he frequently drives her right out of her tree. "I can't be so intensely irritated and then simply turn the irritation off and become relaxed and responsive in bed," she confided. Unfortunately, he irritated her a lot as evenings wore on, so she went to bed exasperated a lot, and their physical intimacy suffered greatly.

The answer to their problem was for them both—especially her—to be direct and in-your-face about the problem. She carefully analyzed when he was at his least irritating. It turned out that on Saturday mornings and after dinner in the evenings his behavior and her feelings were seldom on a collision course. A couple times a week, therefore, they farmed the kids out after dinner. The kids were old enough now that they could sleep over at friends' houses, so that helped. The kids were delighted to do that on Friday nights a couple of times a month, and our friends had the house to themselves on some Saturday mornings.

The improved intimacy mended much in the marriage. In fact, she found his hyperactive ways far less irritating than they had seemed before. Did he change? Not significantly, but she did. And that change made all the difference in their marriage.

There is another aspect of feelings interfering with romance that I see over and over and over in counseling (and now and then in my own life). The two partners have a major disagreement, a fight, a brouhaha, a difference of opinion, an anger match—whatever you want to call it. The ADD spouse marches out the door in a huff, and the non-ADD spouse is churned up, furious. That night, the ADD mate traipses back in the door all brightness and daisies. He or she is ready and eager for sex, as if nothing happened.

The non-ADD mate is devastated. How can this person expect intimacy when the relationship has just been rubbed raw by that fight? The answer is that the ADD spouse has truly forgotten all about the anger, and perhaps even the *subject* of the fight. The ADD spouse is genuinely confused and hurt that the mate is still upset over something that happened hours ago, particularly since that something now seems pretty insignificant. The events of the day have driven the morning's fight (or a fight of the night before) into the background of memory or erased it altogether.

There is a way around this conundrum, but it isn't easy. It is simply immediate communication (nonconfrontational and nonaccusatory if possible). And that's incredibly hard at times, especially for the non-ADD mate.

And communication does not mean simply expressing your hurt in vague terms. You have to paint it in very broad strokes. "I am still angry from the fight we had. I can't get over it as quickly as you do. And I'm certainly in no mood for affection." That's the non-ADD mate's responsibility, to get out into the open what's going on inside.

The ADD mate's responsibility is to accept and honor those feelings. They are genuine. They are painful. And they are hard to understand. The ADD mate cannot sympathize well because ADD people can shed intense emotions readily and quickly. It's alien to an ADD spouse's nature to dwell upon hurts.

There is an important fourth point to remember in sexual communication: avoid doublespeak.

Be Blunt and Clear

Subtlety, innuendo, and suggestion don't cut it in an ADD marriage. If your need is not met or you think something could make your sex life better, you have to spell it out. Both of you.

It's too bad so many married people feel reticent about discussing the incredibly important means that God designed to bring them together and make them one. But in this situation, whether it be two ADD mates or one, precision and clarity are especially necessary. Be direct. Use the technical terms. Draw pictures if need be. Explain. Get the point across.

ADD adults, who thrive on variety and get bored quickly by repetition, are particularly open to new ideas in the area of sexual activity. Here's where a careful balance becomes essential. The non-ADD mate must be willing to perhaps step into the unknown or untried. The non-ADD mate must be ready to draw a line if he or she feels really uncomfortable about a suggestion. The ADD mate must accept such responses as "Not yet," "Not quite," or "No way" without rancor. And the same rules of balance work in the other direction as well, of course.

A good sexual union is an incredibly strong bonding force in marriage. The ADD-influenced marriage, more fragile and volatile than most, needs all the bonding it can get. Clear, direct communication is the only way to achieve that bond.

But communication in marriage goes way beyond just sexual concerns.

Communication Beyond the Bedroom

Jeri speaks:

I was certain that good Christian couples never had arguments. And a good Christian wife did not openly contradict her husband. So Rick and I never fought because fighting takes two and I wouldn't. Rick often hurt me deeply, and I put on this smiling mask and stuffed the hurt. Then I'd hide in the bedroom and pout and throw a pity party. I'd like to say I caught on to the destructiveness of that behavior pretty quickly. Hah. We went on that way for ten years! At the time it seemed easier to nurse my hurt and feel pitiful than to change or challenge him.

Rick speaks:

Thanks to my ADD-disposed gift for being obtuse, I rarely picked up on the signals Jeri sent me. Most people could look at Jeri's facial expression and body language and know immediately that damaging words had just pierced her to the core. Not me. I'd unload, she'd be sweet and placating, and I'd assume it was all over and everything was okay. My need to vent my feelings and my desire to win were served just fine.

I quickly learned that all I had to do was get loud and I controlled the argument. Like so many ADD adults, once I heard the words of conciliation, I'd assume the situation was favorably resolved. I still tend to think that way, but we've both come a long way toward constructively working through our disagreements.

The Burdens of Nature and Nurture

Jeri's childhood was like most people's; if someone yelled at her, she knew that person was angry for some reason. It was natural that she interpreted my loudness as threatening (not physically threatening, but threatening all the same), my forcefulness as anger. To me, being loud and forceful simply meant excitement or urgency. The more I got all stirred up, the louder I became.

I had a vested interest in not seeing the truth about the way my actions affected Jeri. As long as the status quo remained, I won the arguments. That self-interest probably blinded me to her true response as much as anything. It was a bad situation.

Jeri was shaped by her upbringing. We all are. And I was shaped by both ADD and upbringing. It was her nature and nurture to back off. It was my nature to get loud. The only way we could get around our predispositions was to step back when we weren't having a fight and assess our reactions during arguments.

Incidentally, arguments more than anything else in a relationship reveal a lot. They're spontaneous. They come from the heart and head together. If you want to know how you each tick, analyze your arguments.

We could each see that getting past the ways we were both shaped would lead to healthier communication. We eventually worked out some techniques for doing that. Improvement came over time. Here's what we found.

Jeri and I both knew in our heads that our mode of argument—her shrinking back as I exploded—was unhealthy. But that realization has to penetrate to heart level for change to occur. We discussed our arguments during periods of calm, when we could brainstorm rationally and quietly.

When discussing a heavy subject like that, which will require time, you can beat the ADD mate's fleeting attention span by dividing it up. Talk about one aspect of the issue one time, another aspect the next evening, and so on until you get the subject played out. Here the ADD mate must follow the non-ADD spouse's lead. The non-ADD spouse must measure and pace the approach enough to keep the ADD mate's interest piqued.

The means of getting past barriers to communication, such as those erected by nature and nurture, are numerous.

The non-ADD mate tries to be sensitive to an ADD-mate's feelings about control.

"Why should I be sensitive to her needs," the non-ADD mate asks, "when she is so insensitive to mine?"

From a human point of view, that's not a bad question. The answer of course, goes right back to the description of love in 1 Corinthians. Consider also the golden rule. It's not, "Do unto others because they do unto you." Nothing good happens in a marriage (or any other relationship) when the two persons are keeping score.

Control is a big, big issue with ADD adults. We have so little control over so many areas of our life that we grasp every shred of it we can. Then we guard it with everything we have.

Am I overstating the problem? No. Everyone seeks a measure of control in their life, so control becomes an issue in any marriage. In ADD partners' unions, expect it to cause some conflict. Here's how to minimize the problems.

Let's face it. Without Jeri's sound advice and help from time to time, I'd be sunk. I know it. She knows it. I need her steadying hand, her wisdom to tell me when I'm goofing up. Yet when she calls me on some infraction or expresses concern about something I've done or failed to do, I feel threatened. Here's this woman trying to control me.

So I have specifically given her permission to point out the faulty behaviors she sees in me. She phrases her corrections, for example, like this: "You asked me to tell you when you are [riding this subject too hard] [annoying Mrs. Jones] [not finishing the job I asked you to do] [whatever]. Well, you are."

Do you see? By giving her permission, I retain control without losing the value of her insight. And because she reminded me that I had given her permission, she is not nagging. The ADD mate must give this blanket permission to the person whose guidance he or she needs. And the non-ADD spouse must remind the mate of that permission.

Part of the subject of control in a relationship is surprises. I hope the non-ADD mate can understand that as much as ADD folks love variety and spontaneity, we hate surprises. Surprises are beyond the ADD adult's ability to control. Nearly all surprises are nasty to us.

Jeri threw me a surprise birthday party once. She never tried something like that again, but she was really hurt by my cold, even angry response. I walked into this preplanned event and found myself being swept along; everybody but me knew what was supposed to happen next. That was both scary and intimidating. I reacted from the gut, as always, and my reaction was negative.

During the first ten years of our marriage, I got angry if any little thing was changed without my knowledge. Jeri couldn't even rearrange the furniture without torquing me off. It seemed to her, and rightly so, that I had some sort of executive privilege to be spontaneous, changing plans (or furniture layouts) on the spur of the moment, but she did not. In a way, she was right.

We finally figured out that what bothered me was the surprise. Easy fix. Now she simply mentions in advance about some change she's going to make. Using rearranging the furniture as an example, she might say, "I think I'm going to change the furniture around this afternoon." She's not asking permission. She's not testing the waters. She's simply dulling the surprise element.

This kind of solution probably will not be communicated in the course of normal give and take. Often neither spouse understands what's causing the friction between them. Sometimes talking is not the cure-all answer.

In the case above, where Jeri inadvertently scared and intimidated me and I inadvertently spoiled her happiness with my response, talking about it probably would not have brought enlightenment for either of us. It's worth a try—never ever would I suggest you don't even try. But let's assume that in your case, talking it out is fruitless. Even after words pass back and forth, neither of you knows what happened or why.

There are a couple ways to go from there. One is to ask counsel from someone who understands ADD people and can offer insight. Possibly all you need is another person's fresh, objective look at the problem.

Another way to get past such an event is simply to forgive and forget. It happened. It wasn't supposed to go that way. You both regret it didn't go better. Put it away after you forgive each other. Not every lesson in life "takes." Count this situation as one of the ones that didn't.

A third way to resolve your hurt feelings is to consider what you know about each other. In this case, I beg the non-ADD mate to consider his or her spouse's feelings. At the bottom line, I'm talking about allowing your partner some measure of control or choice. The non-ADD mate does not have to remember to do that. Therefore, giving your partner a measure of control, even a small measure, is a love gift meant to promote and heal the union.

But there's a kicker. We ADD mates likely won't notice or appreciate your gift.

A second means of opening up better overall communication deals with giving it time to happen.

Both mates commit to taking time.

Improving communication in an ADD-affected marriage takes lots of time. The ADD adult's brain gets ahead of the mouth, and it seems only natural for the non-ADD adult to take that as a sign that the ADD spouse is either not paying attention or not thinking. I have found it immensely helpful to simply pause as I'm talking and let my thoughts reassemble themselves. Then I continue.

Jeri is especially gracious in giving me the time. She might pause with her own response and wait. That's a signal to me to take time myself.

There's an important reward in this approach. As Scripture says, "Even a fool is thought wise if he keeps silent" (Proverbs 17:28 NIV). Any adult would like to be thought of as wise and deep-thinking. Certainly the ADD adult does, and too often he or she appears the fool simply because of speaking in haste. Not only will the ADD adult sound a lot more sage by deliberately taking extra time, his or her thoughts will be better worked out, better expressed, and more relevant.

This is not to say that such means for improving communication are limited to ADD-tinged marriages. We also benefit from the old standbys that would help any marriage, but we must apply them more diligently.

Use what works for any marriage.

Marriage enrichment seminars and books on marriage offer basic guidelines for enhancing communication. They work in the ADD-affected marriage as well, provided one partner is ready to remind the other partner repeatedly that they're useful.

For starters, I have learned to offer more eye contact. It sounds so simple, so elementary. But to an ADD adult, it's not. And yet most people value it highly for enhancing communication.

It's also good for the ADD mate to rethink body language. My normal pace of conversational body language is at dead run. I'll be talking to someone, either pacing the room or headed for this shelf and that drawer or simply bobbing up and down in place. This much body movement is distracting and sometimes downright insulting to the non-ADD conversationalist.

I've had to exert self-control (a lot of it) to make my body language reflect what I'm really saying. But those two simple changes—eye contact and body language—have made an immense difference in my ability to communicate with Jeri. If the non-ADD mate is put off by the spouse's lack of direct eye contact and body language, say so, by all means. Change is possible.

One old standby that marriage counselors suggest for troubled marriages also works well for the ADD-tinged marriage. In fact, it can work very well *if* the partners remember to use it. They suggest using "I feel" statements. This goes for the ADD and the non-ADD mate both.

Contrast these two statements. Which would raise your hackles less?:

"You never listen to me!"

"I feel like you aren't listening to me."

The first accuses. The second is an it-seems-to-me statement. The first is hyperbolic, the second explanatory.

"Get away from me! Quit yelling!"

"I feel under attack. Please back off."

See the difference?

Another technique for improving communication is echoing, or repeating what your mate said. "I hear you saying that . . ." Along the same lines is asking for reinterpretation. "What are you telling me?"

ADD adults are notorious for not listening and for failing to interpret statements in the same ways non-ADD adults do. I offer couples I counsel an exercise that goes like this: Spouse A asks Question 1 (it can be any question). Spouse B answers in detail and Spouse A cannot interrupt. Now Spouse A repeats what Spouse B just said. The couple reverses the process for Question 2, with Spouse B asking and Spouse A answering. Repeating Jeri's statements in my own words not only helps me understand Jeri better, it keeps me focused. It quells my impulsivity, almost always a good thing when communication is involved. When she repeats what I say, we both gain the confidence that we've gotten the message across in both directions. You may find this technique helps you resolve quite a few communication problems.

Another excellent rule is when one person's voice gets louder, the other's gets softer. This prevents the escalation of emotion and confrontation that so often occurs during communication attempts. I'm not suggesting that Jeri ought to back off when I get hot and heavy. When she responds forcefully but quietly, however, we can keep a discussion a discussion. This is not just an ADD/non-ADD technique. When my son Chip, who also exhibits ADD, and I get into it, the moment one of us raises his voice, the other drops off. It's saved many a discussion from escalating into a nonproductive argument.

There are times when the ADD spouse shouldn't be trying to communicate at all. Sometimes ADD individuals just don't connect well. Very often when we're upset or angry, the best response is no response at all. Back off and settle down. Wait.

It's often hard for ADD folks to compromise, but then that's true of just about anyone. Nevertheless, strive for compromise. It will come easier if you both analyze an issue according to its moral importance and permanence. Will the decision you make affect you forever and ever? A tattoo, for instance, is permanent. A haircut (even a bad one) will grow back. Adultery is a moral issue, and there must be no compromise there. Hair length is not a moral issue, although there was a day when fathers tried to make it one.

Negotiate, then, anything that's not immoral or permanent.

The ADD adult, like the ADD child, needs frequent reminders. In that, I beg the non-ADD adult to remind without sounding angry or patronizing. And you can't do that by simply choosing the correct tone of voice—you have to choose not to *be* angry or patronizing. A patronizing attitude in anyone is pretty hard to take. In a spouse it's really irritating.

Jeri says, "With Chip, who's well into his teen years now, lecturing isn't very effective. It's not desirable anyway; he's almost an adult. I've learned to tell him succinctly what I expect and remind him that I know he is capable and that I want to treat him like the mature young person he is.

"I listen to him and take a genuine interest in what's important to him."

That works well for communication between adults, too.

Finally, when a discussion is really important and must be intense, the ADD adult can take some steps to improve the actual sending and receiving of information. There are several ways to do this.

Sending Clear Messages

Let's assume you two have to discuss something with elaborate implications; what to do about an infirm relative, how to handle a legal problem . . . serious stuff.

Eliminate distractions.

Pick a place without television where peripheral movement and distractions are minimal. We have a couple of places in our house that serve us well. At your house, how about a secluded patio or gazebo? Sitting cross-legged on the bed? In the dining room at the table with the curtains drawn? I've heard of a couple hunkering down in the laundry room with the door closed.

Face each other.

The laundry room couple drags two chairs in beside the washer and dryer and sits down knees to knees. The object of facing each other is to make body language easier for the ADD adult to read. They are literally in each other's face. Intensity goes up sharply, too.

Here's where the ADD adult is going to have to compromise for the sake of a non-ADD listener. ADD mates prefer to be moving around. We talk on the run, do two things at once. This is distracting to a non-ADD conversant. So for once, for a limited time, sit down.

And now it's the non-ADD partner's turn to compromise.

Set a time limit.

This is a real help for the ADD adult. Instead of asking "How long is this going to take?" he says to himself, "There's light at the end of the tunnel." Because our attention span is limited, putting a time limit on the discussion of an important topic both keeps us on course and promises us respite. We don't have to pay attention indefinitely. We don't have to sit still too terribly long. It's comforting to know.

Listen to what you hear, not what you think.

Oh my, this is so hard to do! Especially in an intense conversation. What if Person A doesn't like what he or she hears from Person B? Person A then mentally frames the perfect rebuttal instead of hearing the rest of what Person B is saying. Person A is listening to the inner screaming voice instead of listening to Person B. Person B is probably doing the same thing. The only way to avoid the problem is to recognize it exists and put personal thoughts aside while your spouse is talking. Sometimes it helps to require a pause of ten or twenty seconds between the end of one person's words and the other person's reply. If you know you'll have time to frame a response, you'll be less likely to do it while your mate is talking. (To be honest, when you get going, it's awfully hard to actually do that.)

Give the speaker his or her due.

When your spouse makes a valid point, acknowledge it. When your spouse uses finesse (either person, not just the ADD adult), praise it. This is not a fight, even if it's a fight. It's a struggle to move forward. Help each other.

Avoid opening discussion during HALT.

HALT is Hungry, Angry, Lonely, or Tired. When one mate or both are at diminished capacity, you won't move forward, and moving forward is what any conversation or discussion is all about. It's true that some discussions won't wait until everyone is fed, rested, and relaxed. But when discussion, especially an important discussion, can be commenced under optimal conditions, by all means do so.

Communication is not an achievement. It's a process. It goes on and on, two steps forward and one step back, through the life of the marriage. As you understand the ADD adult's advantages and limitations better, you'll get better at communicating. Slips and misses will still frustrate. Jeri and I, even after all these years, miss frequently.

For that reason, forgiveness must also be a daily process.

Like forgiveness, learning is similarly a daily function of communication. Even when it is ostensibly only for entertainment, communication teaches something. Always. Usually, however, learning and the ADD adult are not good friends. How do you convert communication into degrees and skill attainment? Learning to learn well can do more than anything else to advance the ADD adult. And there are excellent tricks to learning well.

ADDvancing Through School: What the ADD Adult Experienced

Rick speaks:
   I was an MK—a missionary kid. I was always in remedial this and that and special ed courses. Expectations—others' and my own—just kept getting lower and lower. We're talking about failure programmed right in. My teachers' and counselors' reports would all start out, "Rick is a nice boy, but . . ." But.

So many buts. But I wasn't like other kids. But I was never going to amount to a pile of dirt. But I was lazy. But I was dumb. Do kids who are put in the redbirds reading group instead of the bluebirds reading group in the first grade know they're in the dumb bunch? You bet. How do adolescents describe being held back a year in grade school? "I flunked." Negative self-talk is so, so easy for an ADD kid.

I knew about guilt and defeatism from the get-go. ADD kids do. In camp we'd be sent out to sit under a tree and read a Bible passage. I'd be distracted by leaves, birds, clouds, you name it.

We'd get called back in, and I wouldn't have read more than a sentence or two. I'd daydream when I was supposed to be taking a test. I remember once writing down answers to a test without even reading the questions.

My escape from the academic ghetto was basketball. I loved the game. Still do. Most of the time, basketball was the only reason I had for staying in school.

Jeri speaks:

As our son Chip meets the challenges of his life, I grow to appreciate more and more Rick's childhood and I realize how tough it was on him. I don't think a person who has not been labelled learning disordered or Attention Deficit Disordered can really grasp what it's like on the other side of the fence, you might say.

Poor Chip. He tries so hard. He'll read something, but his retention is zip. In math, he can't translate one problem into another. If he's writing, he concentrates either on spelling or on the content of his piece, but he can't handle both at once.

Ten years ago, I would have been incredibly frustrated with a kid like Chip, and I would have taken my frustration out on him. You know, yelling, "It's your fault—you don't try!" Now I realize that as I watch Chip struggle and lose a few and win a few, I'm seeing Rick. This was Rick's world, too, but he didn't win nearly as many as Chip is winning because Rick so very rarely found anyone who believed in him. I can't describe my feelings exactly—a profound sadness, I guess, is the way to say it. I'm sad that Rick had to fight so many battles unsupported.

Praise God we can help Chip learn well. Most of all we can help him keep a brightness, an enthusiasm for life and for learning. Until I got to know Rick, I wouldn't have thought it could be done.

What Learning Differences Are

People who function well with their left brain just don't appreciate how right brainers and ADD adults grew up. And they find it hard to sympathize, let alone empathize. For example, I'll have a young husband tell me about his terrible grade school years. His wife, as much as she would love to be able to get onto his wavelength, shrugs and says, "Yes, but if you had only applied yourself . . ." She doesn't have a clue, and unless she gets one, she's not going to be able to help him much.

I do a lot of marital counseling. Everyone knows learning differences play havoc with self-image, but I don't think many people realize how extensively learning differences affect the rest of a person's life. With surprising frequency, I find some learning disability or attention deficit in one or both partners of a marriage in difficulty. I'd go so far as to say that's almost always the case, at least in part.

Learning

Learning is not just earning grades in school. It's learning about God, about life, about each other, and about the world and how to get along in it. Most people—some teachers, too, for that matter—don't realize that there are two reasons for learning. One is to survive and handle life better, and the other is to be part of the continuum of the human experience. To get along better we need math, languages, geography, and science. Appreciation and absorption of the human experience is why we study philosophy, social sciences, history, and literature.

Learning includes the love of learning. Learning for the sake of learning. A woman learns to crochet, a skill she never had before. Love of learning. A man masters calligraphy, not because he'll use it in his job but because he has always admired the art. Love of learning. A friend reads *Winnie the Pooh* in a Latin translation, just for the fun of it. Love of learning.

Children are pretty much born with a love of learning. New

ideas and new skills may be frustrating or even frightening, but they also fascinate. The child who falls trying to learn to ride a bike learns to ride the bike anyway. For the ADD adult in particular, this principle extends through life.

Learning takes place for better or worse in every situation— at home, at school, away. Children and adults are always absorbing details and impressions. That's learning. We like to think that children learn at school and play at home. That's not so. They play and learn in both places. So do adults. At home, especially, we learn about relationships and life day by day.

Learning Problems

When an adult or child loses that love of learning, you have a problem. You have a problem because that person has given up on herself. And once that happens, the growth ceases. We're born to grow, programmed to grow. Without growth there is no sense of achievement and no happiness. Call it a vague, chronic sense of futility. That sense of futility intensifies and persists through adulthood, causing many problems in interpersonal relationships. In addition there's the very practical difficulty that the person has not acquired the skills and knowledge necessary to move smoothly through life. If your math ability doesn't allow you to balance a checkbook, you're in trouble.

The non-ADD adult has absolutely no concept of what life was like for the ADD mate during childhood. These two adults, trying to forge a union, grew up in alien cultures, even if they were raised in the same neighborhood. What you read in this chapter applies equally to children and adults. I'd like to touch upon children's learning problems in general, because the ADD adult is highly likely to have an ADD kid around the house, and on ADD adults' learning problems in particular. The purpose is to get across to the non-ADD adult what has shaped his or her spouse and what continues to affect that person today. That's the first step in growing beyond the present reality of ADD.

The moment children first lose enthusiasm for learning is the time to seriously question why. Usually, parents start noticing a problem in first or second grade. The problem begins to show when the child is reluctant to go to school. She doesn't like school and doesn't feel good about it. She gets headaches and tummyaches.

Now this is not to say that every time a kid sours on school that he or she should be exhaustively examined. The way a kid feels about school can change from day to day or from year to year. A child might have a dandy kindergarten teacher and an ineffective teacher in first grade, a dazzling third grade and a rotten fourth. Or maybe the child is great in one subject and bombs another. Monitor your child's frustration level. If it increases from year to year and if achievement slides downward, you have to take steps to reverse the trend. By the seventh grade, kids with problems may still be showing up in class physically, but they've already dropped out emotionally and mentally. It is extremely hard then to get them to succeed. You've got almost-adults who are not growing and, unless someone or something turns them around, will never grow.

So if as parents you see that within the first few years of school, your child's interest has flagged and he is starting to fall behind, do something. Find out what the problem is. The question you need to answer is this: Are we dealing with a learning problem or a lazy kid?

Your kids won't outgrow learning difficulties, whether they be ADD or some other problem. You had best tackle learning problems early by teaching different learning techniques and dealing with attention problems. Tackling problems early is the best way to avoid difficulty in the long haul. The parent who expects a child to change spontaneously or outgrow difficulties is probably in for a disappointment.

Frankly, lazy teens probably exist. Lazy grade-schoolers probably don't. Most young kids invest a lot of time and effort into school. If they aren't getting a payoff, they know it, even if that knowledge is below the conscious level. They back off; they appear lazy. If parents don't deal with the problem, these kids grow into "lazy" adults. Some adults have given up completely.

They know they're stupid because everyone's been telling them so.

Adults then are considered super-lazy. "He'd learn if only he wanted to," people around him assert. The reasoning here, you see, is that since he appears normal on the outside, the inside must be normal as well. Therefore, laziness or stubbornness is to blame for any failure or inability to learn.

In the Minirth Meier New Life Clinic, we're faced with the question of learning difficulties versus laziness all the time. Sometimes it's a "lazy kid." Sometimes it's an adult so totally frustrated by life that he or she is seeking some kind of help. What's going on with this person who isn't functioning well? How do we deal with it? These are the questions every non-ADD spouse of an ADD mate deals with daily.

Dealing with ADD's effects on learning can cause intense frustration until you develop some means of overcoming the problems. Obviously, you're not going to get far until both mates can see precisely what the problems are.

IDENTIFYING LEARNING PROBLEMS

An acquaintance of mine named Bill found out at the age of fifty-one that he is dyslexic. It came as quite a surprise to him. He still wouldn't know if it weren't for his kids.

Now Bill (not his real name, I bet you've guessed) has books all over his house. He spends much time reading, but he reads very slowly—somewhere around 180 words a minute. His wife also reads constantly. So their daughters grew up among books with parents who appreciate books. The girls had some reading problems very early on. They both learned to read at home around age five. But their mom didn't recognize the signs of dyslexia (the girls transposed numbers and reversed letters, for example). So they sort of worked their way around their problems and read tons of books as they grew up.

Bill's job requires extensive reading and writing, and it takes him a long time. He figured he was just a slow reader. Then his girls, now in early adulthood, became aware of the fact they had been compensating for some serious learning differences. Their mom, who reads about a thousand words per minute (the high side of average), never had problems.

But the girls knew that their father had always read slowly. "Hey, Pop," said the eldest, "we figured out where our reading gene came from."

It's not hard to believe that Bill had struggled in school with academics. He accepted the prevailing wisdom of his day that his problems were all due to poor study habits. He recollects, "I remember one day in high school, I decided I was going to really sit down and start studying. I arranged all my books and papers and pencils on the desk, settled myself in the chair, and . . ." He pauses. "The fire sirens went off all over town. An old church down the street was on fire, and the whole town turned out to stand around all night watching. There went my study resolve."

Bill illustrates the prevailing situation: kids who have trouble in school are often blamed for that trouble. Bill was not hyperactive, but he daydreamed a lot. He was frequently accused of not listening. He was polite and quiet and all the things parents like to see in kids, but his difficulties with class work were still identified as being his fault somehow.

No one then, and too many educators now, understood that Bill's brain spontaneously flitted. Certain neurons failed to fire and he'd tune out. Then random neurons would fire, sending his thoughts (which are all controlled by neuron activity, of course), into unexpected, unwanted directions. What was happening in his brain was beyond Bill's ability to control.

There is a sad postscript to Bill's story. He has heard so long that he could improve his reading if he would only apply himself that he cannot quit believing it even now. Despite what his wife and daughters tell him to the contrary, he feels that somehow it's his fault. He is still ashamed of his reading skills, unable to realize that he has moved mountains to get where he is today.

Bill's situation is typical. He has unconsciously learned to compensate for his learning difficulty, and he gets along pretty well. But how much smoother and happier his life would have gone if his problems had been identified as problems rather than character flaws and addressed correctly early on.

ADD is diagnosed pretty much the same way in adults as it is in kids, with this big advantage: the adult realizes what's at stake and cooperates well. Perhaps *takes an active part in the diagnosis* would be a better phrase than *cooperates well*. It also helps that the ADD adult's spouse and friends know him or her well and have observed him or her over a long period of time; they can offer insights about that adult that they would not have regarding a child.

One of the first things we might ask when evaluating an adult is, "What were your grade school report cards like?" We ask how the adult remembers school as well, but this answer is not as telling as the written record because it comes from the subject's perspective. It's important for our purposes to know what the teachers (and perhaps the principal) saw in this person. Keep in mind, however, that for most adults, these observations were made before educators had any kind of ADD awareness.

Let's pretend that Bill's "then" is actually "now," and he is a grade-schooler being evaluated for learning problems instead of being told he has lousy study habits. What ought his parents be doing and looking for? And remember that although I may say *child* for convenience's sake, I mean any person. Adults are just as likely to benefit from evaluation.

BEWARE OF TEST SCORES

Learning differences, both the helpful ones (exceptionally bright kids) and deleterious ones (kids with serious problems), are not alien conditions. They are merely the extremes of the normal learning spectrum. The "breakoff points" on that spectrum are identified by numbers. (Breakoff points are used in every form of assessment to identify predetermined conclusions, e.g., a score from 90 to 100 is an A.) When a person scores above a certain number, he or she is placed in a different category from the person whose score is a numeral or two below that number.

Tests are artificial measurements of learning, but parents and testers often fail to realize that. The person who earns one point above breakoff is often no brighter than the person who scored one point below breakoff, but one has "passed" and one has "flunked." This arbitrary designation persists right through a student's whole lifetime. Test results can scar the confidence of a person terribly. Be extremely wary, therefore, about using test results as the sole means of evaluation.

Recognize also that nearly any test presents a stressful situation, and kids *and* adults with learning problems tend to handle a stressful situation of that sort poorly. In addition, people with learning difficulties generally have trouble with multiple choice, and that's the form of many standardized tests. To offer an extreme example, let's say a blind person with a PhD is forced to take a test under standardized conditions. If the conditions do not include verbal responses or Braille, that brilliant holder of an earned doctorate will flunk. He'll get a zero. Learning differences are exactly the same kind of handicap when it comes to testing.

Evaluation requires a detailed analysis of each person, child or adult, identifying eccentricities (we all have them!) and differences. We all have differences, too. In fact, some psychologists go so far as to say everyone has learning disabilities because no two people can learn in the same ways. Probably a fourth of the kids in today's classroom, like Bill, are having trouble with the present curriculum. The presentation of information is not geared to the ways they learn. So look carefully at the whole person, whether test scores indicate some problem or not.

Don't Believe in Laziness

How often did my parents and caretakers hear, "The only problem is that little Rick doesn't care. If you will just punish him for laziness and be strict—impose good, solid discipline—you will make him a better student. That will solve the problem."

Let me tell you, little Rick was trying his level best. He could not be "made into" a better student, as if the caregiver need only pinch the clay in the right places. Punishment and rigidity just make a bad situation infinitely worse.

Parents, never take someone else's word that your kid is lazy! And spouses, I hope you won't glibly accept that diagnosis about your mates, either.

One of the biggest problems with a simplistic diagnosis determining that the child is merely lazy and undermotivated, apart from the fact it's almost always dead wrong, is its fatal implication that you can forget about other problems. It's a lot easier to dump responsibility on the kid than it is to keep looking for more complex reasons. Sure, laziness exists. But it is a diagnosis made by exclusion. You eliminate every other possibility first.

Eliminate Abusive Elements

A person on drugs or a person who drinks too much, be that person young or old, is impaired. That person can't think effectively. He can't create well (although he may believe otherwise). He can't react quickly or do things well. Any substance abuse problem must be addressed first before evaluation or improvement can begin. You won't do anything positive until the influence of that substance or substances is out of the picture.

Do small kids have drug problems? Sometimes. All people need to feel success. People with learning difficulties don't have that feeling. Worse, it seems as if no one understands. Particularly at risk are the learning-challenged kids in their teens. They're impulsive anyway, and they feel the pain of routine failure and a sense of worthlessness. One way or another, they are going to reduce that pain and find some relief. Drugs and alcohol are available to all our kids in this culture.

Get a Broad Picture

When you're trying to identify learning differences in either a child or an adult, everyone involved with that person should have some input.

In Bill's case his wife lit up like Christmas. "Of course! It never occurred to me that you might be mildly dyslexic. But that would explain the way you have trouble with phone numbers unless they're repeated, and the slow reading pace."

Their eldest daughter added her opinion. "I've always had trouble with spelling. Spell check on the computer is the greatest thing that was ever invented. You claim you're a poor speller because you didn't pay attention in school. Wouldn't dyslexia and a mild attention deficit be a better explanation?"

Their youngest daughter said, "Now we know why you hate Scrabble. When everyone sits down to a Scrabble game, you head for the garage to sharpen garden tools or something. Hey, no problem; the tools can use sharpening. But, Dad, you always seem so down on yourself, as if you're ashamed you don't like Scrabble."

If you're trying to identify a learning difficulty, encourage your family to participate in this same way. If you're evaluating a child talk to her teachers. Get your pediatrician's insight. In the case of a child or an adult, consult skilled specialists. Invite your friends, relatives, and neighbors to coffee and pick their brains.

And most of all, listen to your kid or adult. Observe closely. Does the person:

- give up easily?
- get angry or frustrated easily?
- get bored easily when read to?
- play with a number of toys in quick succession and then complain of having nothing to do?

- daydream a lot?
- persist in defiance or disobedience, testing the limits?
- keep moving constantly?
- flit from interest to interest rapidly?
- get into scrapes or experience physical injury because of failure to "look before you leap"?
- do strange or unpredictable things a lot?
- consistently shout when shouting is unnecessary?

Every normal person, child or adult, exhibits some of the behaviors above. But clusters of such behaviors suggest some learning difference or difficulty. Please note that the list above is intended to alert you to possibilities and seek out other help. It is not intended to be a diagnostic tool.

Emphasize this point from the beginning with your ADD mate or child and drive it home over and over: if there turns out to be a problem, that problem is *not* the person. There's something else going on. I guarantee it. Bill finds it impossible to absorb that message because he heard the opposite message his whole life. Get the word to your child early!

DEALING WITH LEARNING DIFFICULTIES

Bill was never evaluated for learning problems. When he attended the early grades, educators and parents didn't know about such things. By the time educators were catching on and starting to consider innate learning differences and difficulties, he was in high school. Besides, even now children who do not have a behavior problem are rarely evaluated. So long as little Bill sits quietly in his seat, he's perceived as being okay and needing no help.

The object of any pursuit of learning differences is to improve learning. That's usually reflected as improved grades or even, in the case of an adult, improved pay or recognition. The first step in attempting to improve learning, then, is to find out what needs changing.

Evaluate!

Today we know that evaluation is the first step. By that I mean a thorough professional evaluation, not a passing opinion offered by a school counselor. The purpose of the evaluation is to find out exactly how the person can learn best and what learning techniques will not work. From that you build a learning strategy, a game plan.

This requires that adults, children's parents, and teachers sit down together and work out a course of action. In the case of an adult, the whole family is involved. It may cost parents and others extra time, and time is a commodity in dreadfully short supply at this stage of a family's life. Time is an investment you must make to evaluate accurately.

The ADD adult usually cannot evaluate herself. The evaluation must come from outside, particularly from someone well versed in identifying learning problems and differences. Here the non-ADD spouse must take the lead. It is the non-ADD spouse who will first see that learning problems can exist and can be corrected—the light at the end of the tunnel shines first in the non-ADD mate's eyes.

If the ADD adult refuses a professional evaluation, the non-ADD mate ought do the best he can to identify ways to help the ADD spouse learn. This chapter and the next will describe such ways.

Dedicate the Time Required

I often compare raising ADD kids to growing grass in the sand. Anyone who's tried growing grass in sand knows that sand is soft, it dries out quickly, and it carries very little nourishment. To get grass to grow well there, you have to water constantly. You have to fertilize frequently because nutrients flush away in the loose substrate. And you have to protect your grass, lest too many feet and too much use crush it out of existence. It's a lot of effort for an achievement that would be so much easier in other soil.

ADD kids and adults need constant fertilization and watering in the sense that we require the time and efforts of others. We need praise, reinforcement, guidance, and structure. We need protection, too. We too often go galloping off without thinking ahead, without counting the cost or risks. We need a steady hand and head to rein us in occasionally. All that care and protection requires time. Given the extra nurturing and protection we need, we develop as smooth a growth of turf as does any other lawn.

Part of the time should be spent in periodic reevaluation, like checking for yellow spots in the lawn. What works and what won't? What does the ADD child or adult need at this stage of life that he doesn't have right now? What forgiveness and what praise are due? What should be the strategy tomorrow? What decisions are next?

When Bill was in third grade, he was getting the same poor grades as was a friend, David. But David was a problem child, what they used to call a juvenile delinquent. David flunked because of his poor grades. Bill, who went woolgathering a lot but was otherwise a "nice," well-behaved boy, was promoted in spite of his poor grades. In retrospect, we have a pretty good idea that for both boys, it was the wrong decision.

This brings up a third aspect of dealing with learning differences. The non-ADD mate will have to discard some learning methods, no matter how much she loves them for herself.

Avoid What Doesn't Work

Frequently, a grade-school teacher will assert that a child is having problems because of immaturity. "Let's give him another year and he'll be fine." In other words, hold him back.

Almost always, one more year doesn't make it better. It merely piles self-concept problems on top of the learning difficulty. Elementary educators don't often see long-term results because the results are not obvious for years. As the grown child looks back, however, "held back" becomes "flunked."

People with legitimate learning differences don't need more

of the same. Those study techniques, the methods of absorbing information, didn't work in the first place. They won't work in the second place. The learner needs something different.

That is just as true of adults. Bill is not going to improve his reading skills (or his Scrabble prowess) by doing the same things he did in grade school and high school. Reading against a timer won't do it. He's already tried that as part of a speed-reading course.

Scanning won't help. He tried over and over to master scanning. He says, "My eyes will start down the page, and it's just like they trip. They stumble over a word and go scooting and tumbling to the bottom of the page like Jack and Jill. And my brain doesn't pick up a single word that my eyes are bouncing over on the way down."

Incidentally, it happens that running his finger along a line to keep his eyes moving along that line does work. Visibly embarrassed, Bill shakes his head. "How would it look for a grown man to point to the words with his finger as he reads? Naaa." Do you hear what Bill is really saying even though he doesn't realize it? My early grade school teachers called that a crutch and wouldn't let me do it. And the stigma about doing it has stuck for over forty years. It's important to remove the stigma of "crutches" and to encourage whatever works. It doesn't matter how it looks. Most of Bill's reading takes place in private. If he's self-conscious, let him refrain from pointing in public.

In short, for starters, the person young or old who is looking for improvement might try altering simple things. When that doesn't do the job, we go on to more elaborate solutions. The game plan could be fairly simple; it might be extremely complex. Let's look in detail at ways to make learning work for ADD kids, ADD adults, and others.

These strategies are general approaches that apply to both kids and adults with ADD disadvantages. In a separate chapter I'll define some strategies for upper-level studies—high school and college—that can help ADD students.

Find Out What Works and Use It

Bill's big stumbling block was his own attitude. He didn't think much of his family's assessment of his reading and learning problems. To him everything they said was all just another platter of barbecued Spam. His teachers had been right. If only he'd applied himself better and hadn't had lazy study habits . . .

Modify attitudes.

Here's where the mate of an ADD adult can really help.

Bill might be able to get past his attitude of helplessness with some strong, no-nonsense self-talk. "My wife and kids are sharp, and they know about these things. I can trust their assessment." "Teachers and their opinions aren't perfect." "I can do it if I try other ways of learning." That self-talk would then be reinforced by support and encouragement from family and friends.

ADD kids and adults don't think and act in abnormal ways. They think and act in normal ways to a greater extreme than do most folks. Nowhere does this show up better than in the area of support. Everyone needs some support in order to keep going well. ADD folks need massive doses of it.

The spouse of an ADD adult, especially a left-brain oriented spouse, also needs more encouragement than do most people. That person is not used to bucking the tide constantly in the swim through life. Continual struggle is intensely draining to a person who is not accustomed to it.

A part of feeling successful is to see the tasks you spend your time on come to completion. In order to see and relish success as an ADD-influenced person, you may have to break down large tasks into a series of smaller ones and triumph step by step.

Let's illustrate with little Bill. He's back in grade school, faced with a whole page of subtraction problems. Children who complete the page with three or fewer errors get gold stars. Children who complete the page with four to six errors get silver stars. Bill doesn't complete the page. No star for him.

Let's pretend that Bill has an enlightened teacher who understands about wandering attention. She wants to promote stick-to-itiveness in Bill. So she gives him a silver star for every line completed correctly and a gold star if he completes the paper at all. She keeps an eye on him and sticks that silver star on the worksheet the moment he completes the row. Instant gratification does wonders for an ADD person. When Bill finishes the page, she announces, "Like all of us at one time or another, Bill occasionally needs help finishing. Today he did it on his own and he did it splendidly!" Praise. Ah, praise! We ADD folks hunger for recognition. We'll find a way to earn negative recognition if there is no positive recognition forthcoming. The teacher's acknowledgment of Billy's accomplishment is an immense boost. He's the center of attention for doing something good. That message sticks, believe me.

A spouse can do that, too. Break a task into smaller units and liberally recognize when those units are successfully completed. Take yard work, for example. There's mowing the front, mowing the back, trimming the hedge, weed-whacking along the fence, washing and refilling the birdbath, pulling the grass in the flower bed, and deadheading the roses. A left brainer sees that as one extensive task. The ADD adult does well to recognize a dozen tasks there. A non-ADD spouse can wait to see if her scattershot husband will finish all that and then criticize if he does not, or she can verbally recognize the completion of each sub-task. Guess which approach produces the desired result, which in this case is simply getting all the yard work done.

Another thing that almost always works to enhance learning in ADD individuals is to change the immediate environment to something more conducive to learning.

Modify surroundings.

There are no easy answers to ADD problems, but this is one of the least difficult: positioning.

For example, little Bill did poorly when he sat next to the pencil sharpener, which was attached to the wall near the windows. He did much better when he sat at a desk on the far side of the room. No one noticed the difference, unfortunately, and he spent a lot of months by the sharpener. The windows presented a distraction; windows are magnets for daydreamers. But the pencil sharpener was a distraction as well. Whenever some kid appeared out of nowhere and started cranking away with that unique grinding sound, there went Bill's concentration.

Some ADD people should be sitting right next to the boss, or the speaker, or the teacher, or the action, or whatever's the focus of interest. Others need a lot of visual information about what's going on, and they profit from sitting at the back of the room or the far end of the table.

Putting a child or a young adult into a smaller class with different curriculum can sometimes make all the difference. Fortunately, ADD adults trying to remedy past educational lacks can pick and choose from various curricula and learning methods to find one that works. Most school kids can't, which makes parents' intervention so crucial.

When I intend to read Scripture, which takes concentration, meditation, and discipline, I retreat into a cubicle with blank walls and no distractions. I have to. It's the only way to tackle complex concepts. I have to be careful where I position my desk. Am I facing a blank wall or a window? It makes all the difference. As the realtor and shopkeeper say, location is everything.

What you do within the modified environment isn't quite so easy to manipulate. But modifying methods sure helps.

Modify methods and habits.

When Bill points with a finger as he reads, he is employing what his teachers used to call a crutch. They pronounced the word *crutch* with the same contempt they used for words like *grave robber* and *truancy,* as if a crutch were an odious thing.

Think about crutches. If it weren't for them, a lot of unfortunate people couldn't get around at all. Sometimes you heal and no longer need a crutch, or you outgrow it. But for a lot of disabled folks, that crutch will always be there. No one blames a disabled person for going through life on crutches. If you need the crutch, you need it!

Compensatory methods such as Bill uses could fall in the same category as eyeglasses and hearing aids. Without glasses, Bill would be a menace on the highway. With them, he's an excellent driver. Without new reading strategies, he's crippled. With them, he can do more things better and faster.

One of the best ways to improve reading is by reading. That's true of just about any other activity as well. Simply repeating more of the same thing may not be the best route to improvement, however. For example, rereading something isn't going to do much. That's just more of the same. Rather, the smart reader will try out the active reading techniques schools and learning labs suggest, using what works and discarding what doesn't.

Most adults, ADD or otherwise, don't have reading strategies. But everyone needs them. Reading is how to get the information we all want or need. Under what conditions can you read best? Figure them out. Are you a scanner, skipping along, or do you take each word in turn? Is that the fastest way *you* can handle it? Remember, everyone is different. We're not talking about what "everyone" does, or what your spouse does. Right now we're talking about you. ADD adults whose reading is slow or halting may find that they are auditory learners; taped books might be the answer for them. Libraries carry an immense array of taped material.

Some ADD adults profit from being read to—an activity which can profit the reader, usually the non-ADD mate, as well. If the non-ADD mate can read in a moving vehicle (it makes some people carsick), make long drives a learning time. Driving in the car is a good time to listen to taped books also. Read aloud after dinner or on relaxing Sunday afternoons. Pick specific times, if possible.

A very necessary modification is changing the way children and adults take tests. The person who would do very poorly on a written examination might reverse fortune and do splendidly were he or she to take the test verbally. Most educators, drivers' license examiners, and such don't have time to administer a test orally, however.

If you have an ADD child or high school student, or if you are an ADD college student, how about working out a deal between you, the instructor, and the parents or spouse of another auditory learner? With the instructor's support, you read the tests to the student who's not related to you, and your partner parent or spouse can administer tests orally to your favorite auditory learner. Many ADD kids and adults know a lot they can't write on paper. With this kind of arrangement, everybody wins. At least two ADD kids have a better chance at measurable success. And the instructor can point to teaching success.

Very often, however, ADD adults and children simply cannot make these modifications on their own. Their own physiology turns against them, you might say, preventing them from functioning the way they want to and know they need to. It's time to look at modifications of behavior itself.

Modify behavior.

People with ADD have a strong tendency to attract punishment, and hyperactive people with ADD face lots and lots of punishment. The ADD adult is used to that fact, having experienced the phenomenon since childhood. It's a life-style the non-ADD spouse simply cannot appreciate. Grown-ups are universally certain that children exhibit the symptoms of ADD simply to be perverse or obstinate and that a little heavy-handed discipline will drive that nasty streak right out of them. Just ask me, I know.

And I'll be the first to admit that the behavior of a lot of ADD people is downright irritating. There are two possible corrections for the more objectionable aspects of ADD behavior, and neither of them is punishment. One is managing the person's surroundings and the other is medication. Diet, for some kids but usually not for adults, is a possible third way.

Manage Surroundings

Managing the ADD person's surroundings means limiting the situations that predictably cause trouble for that person. He may want to do something or go somewhere, but that doing or going is unwise. It's not easy; it chafes to be denied a wish like that.

For example, if a person, particularly a child, gets easily overstimulated and goes ballistic in unusual situations, it pays to minimize those situations. Let's say that I do not function well in crowds. That's true of some ADD individuals. So I must keep contact with crowds as minimal as possible. That means staying home from the mall on Saturday; it means watching parades on television even if I live in Pasadena.

ADD people are more hyperactive some days than others. Those days are not predictable, but they must be taken in stride. Perhaps you are a hyperactive high school student who usually goes swimming after school on Mondays and Wednesdays. This is Monday, but today happens to be one of your bad days, so you may not want to head for the swimming pool. Your history has shown that going to the pool is extremely stimulating. If you go, you're going to drive your mom straight to China tonight with your behavior, and you'll both end up furious and frustrated. In the interest of peace, you abstain. It's not easy, but you know that the payoff—a peaceful evening—is worth it.

Another modification is to provide structure to the person's life. This consists of limiting free, unstructured time, and in a child's case, supervising even free time closely. ADD kids generally don't do well without an umpire. They need someone looking down from above. Parents and teachers serve that primary role, and coaches, spouses, and business mentors serve that purpose in later life. You'd be surprised how many of us ADD adults need exactly that same thing. A non-ADD spouse serves as the perfect mentor because of the intimate relationship. Others who can help might be a pastor or a respected family friend.

You can't send a bunch of ADD kids out into the woods to play fort by themselves. They'll be squabbling in nanoseconds. Let an older child go along to referee arguments and provide direction, and ADD kids can build a splendid, beautiful fort. Our behavior will settle if we're under a wise, guiding hand. This does not end with adulthood.

ADD children need structure during summer vacation also. ADD adults also need structure during vacation and during holiday times. In fact, we need it even more then because we don't have the structure of daily routine, going to work, and school to focus our efforts. The need for rules and limits does not end when the school door closes.

Supervision is not the only control on behavior. Some people tout diet as a calming or stimulating influence—the kind of foods taken in. The hoopla over what is called the Feingold diet has pretty much abated, but once upon a time, twenty years ago, it was highly controversial. Its supporters claimed that changes in diet could turn a wild child into a tame puppy. Detractors said it was medical hocus-pocus to think that basic foods such as tomatoes were culprits in aberrant behavior when millions of people can eat them and remain unaffected. Enough research has since been completed that we can see the effects of diet more clearly. Statistically across the population as a whole, dietary changes make no difference. But there is a small group of people for whom manipulating diet really does work. For them, it pays to cut out the suspect foods and obtain the lost nutrients some other way.

Be advised that simplistic solutions, such as removing sugar and tomatoes from a person's diet, are ill-advised. It's never that easy. Never.

Medication is the other avenue.

Medication

Medication is not a simple answer either. Neither is it a cure-all. Administering certain stimulants to hyperactive children settles them down. Apparently, these medications can work similarly for most adults as well. Ritalin is the most commonly used of these drugs. Others include Trofanil, Cylert, Imiparine, and Dexadrine. A new product, Adderal, was shown in a clinical evaluation to be effective in treating ADD.

Because Ritalin has been around for some time, we have been able to study its effects longitudinally—that is, over a span of years. Apparently, side effects are minimal and adults who were treated as children seem to suffer no problems from the drug.

But what about continuing medication through adulthood? Generally speaking, modifying behavior and attitude with an eye to improving attention is a better route. But for some adults, the brain connections never reach a level the adult wants. That person may want to consider medication.

Drugs can decrease impulsivity and distraction. To that extent, medication improves the atmosphere which promotes concentration. Able to concentrate better, the person is able to perform better. Sometimes the person achieves academic success that eluded him or her in the past. Success builds upon success, confidence upon confidence.

It's an issue you have to weigh on a case by case basis. One therapist has been quoted as saying that he saw an adult poet who could not write poetry when she was on Ritalin. On the other hand, another woman was absolutely enthralled by the changes medication allowed her. For the first time in her marriage—in her life—she could sit still long enough to listen to, for instance, what her husband had done at work that day. She was finally able to focus.

In one sense, drugs are a quick fix. Ritalin and others take hold quickly and wear off quickly. The child who goes to school medicated in the morning probably comes home wired at three.

The drugs do not seem to be habit-forming or dangerous in themselves.

Serious dangers unrelated to the drug itself lurk, however. One great danger in parent and child alike is unrealistic expectations. Every adult and child wishes, dreams, insists that the drug can and will work a miracle and suddenly bluebirds will sing, flowers will bloom, and the kid will earn a Rhodes scholarship.

A drug regimen does not automatically improve school, work, or any other activity. You see, too often ADD is diagnosed in kids as if it were the only thing wrong. It almost never is. Other factors are at work as well. Reduce the ADD signs and symptoms that were overshadowing those other factors, and they emerge. Testing is not finished once ADD is diagnosed. In order to really help the child, you have to find the other problems as well.

ADD kids and their parents attach so many expectations to the drug that if it fails to produce good grades, the child is blamed. "You're being treated. Why don't you shape up?" parents may say. And the kids may wonder the same thing.

Another danger is that the ADD child on medication will melt into the woodwork. There's a big, big difference between behaving and learning. The child may be sitting still at last, even appearing to pay attention. But the child's memory is still impaired, the synapses are still not firing the way other people's do. And because the child is no longer a nuisance, her teachers may not notice that her learning has not improved. The kid suffers years of poor learning and retention, virtually ignored.

The ADD adult who as a child took these medications must keep all the above in mind. The ADD adult's agonizing question, "What's wrong with me?" might be answered right here. The medication did not work a miracle. It simply modified external behavior. How disappointing it is when the ADD adult learns that reality late in life!

Medication is a valuable tool for managing ADD. It is not indicated for other learning differences.

There is a reason doctors treating ADD patients constantly alter medication dosages and take people off them altogether. Many children outgrow their hyperactivity and lack of concentration as their nervous systems mature and neurotransmitters stabilize. Most doctors, therefore, prescribe Ritalin or other drugs for a limited time. They might put the child on the drug for several months, then take the child off and see how behavior fares. If the child is outgrowing the hyperactivity, there's no need to go back to drug management. Usually, the time off from a drug regimen takes place during summer vacation when the child is not in school.

However, doctors may let the child remain on medication if the kid is such a wall-climber that he will be hobbled socially without it. Also, families traveling on extended vacations may want the child on medication at least for the duration of the trip. No harm is done in such cases.

All this, you see, does not mean that someday for certain, the person will be free of the need. Most will be. The vast majority, in fact, will be. But some will not.

The July 18, 1994 issue of *Time* magazine tells of a gentleman in Michigan who was diagnosed as ADD at age 54. He medicated himself inadvertently, as it were, by drinking, literally, hundreds of ounces of coffee daily. Thirty or forty cups. The caffeine, a stimulant, helped him settle down—the same thing Ritalin, Adderal, and others do. It was not a cure-all by any means. In his first twelve years of marriage, the article claims, he went through fifteen jobs. He lost his driver's license for a year when distractions garnered him too many traffic tickets. His regret? He wonders what his life and his family's lives could have been, had he been diagnosed and treated effectively.

Obviously, ADD adults don't magically turn into left brainers once they're old enough to vote. Let's consider other aspects of dealing with learning difficulties throughout life.

FOUR

ADDvancing Through the School of Life: Effective Learning

Jeri speaks:

You know how you really want your kid to be excellent and beautiful and bright and perfect? Everyone imagines the little baby growing up, acing college, becoming a Rhodes scholar, opening a professional practice, and presenting the dreamer with lots of brilliant little grandchildren. And then the reality of ADD sets in, and professionals tell you your kid is never going to make it to college. Best to teach him or her a trade that doesn't need brains.

I accepted that prevailing philosophy at first, along with the rest of the world. I know better now. Now that I've watched Rick struggle and succeed and as I watch Chip come up through school triumphant, I'm certain that most ADD people belong in college. Think how much raw talent this country needs, and how much of it is blocked off by traditional prejudices about ADD!

I see and fight those prejudices constantly as I stand by Chip on his way through life. And Rick. Imagine my shock when I learned that Rick, who is bright and successful and articulate, grew up as a failure in the making. And because I've never walked in his shoes, I'll probably never fully realize what it took for him to get where he is. I stand in awe anyway.

Rick speaks:
School would have been just about the neatest thing in the world if it weren't for having to learn. All those lessons really messed up my public school experience.

I'm speaking facetiously from my adult viewpoint, of course, but back when I was in grade school, it actually did seem that way. Most of my teachers gave up on me. I irritated adults even though I didn't want to. I just didn't know how not to—and I irritated most of the other kids, too. My teachers and parents battled desperately to make me the same as other kids—that is, academically bright and attentive—and they consistently lost the fight. I was destined to end up stuck in some entry-level job that opened up only because the trained chimp that formerly held the position got promoted.

What the Advanced ADD Student Faces

I read an estimate once that 70 percent of Americans would benefit from college. Of course, I read another estimate somewhere else that asserted the figure was 40 percent. Obviously, these two estimators were calculating in different factors. No matter. The bottom line is, a lot of adults could do better in life by continuing their education beyond high school.

In fact, that's what many adults are doing. Enrollment in the adult education and continuing learning courses that many community colleges offer is mushrooming. And how about the man who finds himself forced out of a job in his forties, or the woman, divorced or widowed, who discovers herself in a job marketplace she's never been in before? These people *must* chart new learning waters. And then, of course, there are the seniors, people who are retired or nearly so and want to pursue new interests.

The number of ADD people among those ranks is no different from the numbers anywhere else. We all, sooner or later, are faced with the opportunity for advanced learning. The ADD adult too often doesn't even consider the opportunity. "I'm no good at school stuff." "Wish I could, but I can't." "Are you kidding? Me?"

ADD adults get into higher learning for another reason: we are notoriously late bloomers. We didn't do well in grade school and high school, so we don't much like school. Some of us get held back, so that we're late graduating—if we graduate at all. A lot don't. And we are slow to become aware of our own potential. When others are completing college around age twenty-one or twenty-two, we're just getting started, looking at a graduation date maybe five years away.

The ADD adult who would really like to learn new skills, to pursue new knowledge, needs the non-ADD mate desperately. The ADD spouse needs the non-ADD mate's constant encouragement. But on top of that, the non-ADD spouse can encourage new study techniques and learning skills. Do ADD adults read books like this? Not often. The non-ADD mates are the readers. Similarly, the non-ADD mates can lead their spouses into whole new horizons of learning. We ADD folk probably will never cross those horizons if our spouses or others close to us don't help us there. Here are some ways to go about it.

Seeing the Picture

You already know about the factors going against ADD kids in school. ADD kids irritate whether they're hyperactive or not. Many adults falsely assume the child is acting out deliberately.

"Settle down! Stop running around." The kid doesn't. The adult gets torqued. Over and over.

And of course the squirming, running, climbing, making

noise, bumping things, kicking rhythmically, or pounding on something is a nuisance. People don't like living inside a popcorn popper, and that's how it feels when a hyperactive kid is on the loose.

Many ADD adults irritate just as much. They are constantly moving. They can't sit still, can't pace themselves, can't go about business quietly. Note I'm not saying that they refuse to. I'm saying that they physically cannot.

For example, the cordless phone is the niftiest invention, created just for me. When I'm on the phone, I pace. I fidget. I'm constantly moving. I really need either that cordless model or a phone with a very long cord. I've never outgrown the constant activity of my childhood.

Hyperactivity is not the whole source of problems. Even when hyperactivity is not part of the picture, ADD people don't end up in anyone's good graces. Sure, they sit there. But they can't turn out the work. So the people around them accuse them of not caring or of being lazy. The only difference between a hyperactive person and a sedentary person is that the sedentary person is quickly forgotten. The hyperactive person won't let himself be forgotten.

The ADD person learns differently. We call him a *kinesthetic learner*. That's a person, child or adult, who must learn by means other than those employed in most traditional schools. Kinesthetic learners learn through motion, not when they're sitting at a desk. Neither lecture nor rote memorization nor drills work worth beans for such learners. Most schools lean heavily on those methods because they are the easiest to carry out when one teacher is giving information to twenty-five or thirty kids. But the kinesthetic learner obtains knowledge and understanding only through hands-on learning or movement of some kind.

By college, the kinesthetic learner is way out in left field because higher education emphasizes lecture, memorization, and drill. The ADD student is odd person out right there.

Picture a city—let's take Dallas, for instance. How can you

get into Dallas? I suppose you could canoe up the Trinity River but not many do. Wings or wheels are more practical. There's the train. Bus service from other cities will dump you out at the station downtown. You can fly into Dallas-Fort Worth International and take the shuttle to town. (The airport, for those of you who've not been here, is a few miles west of town.) You can drive. Regardless whether you take the plane, bus, or car, you'll come in on a road—Interstate 75, I-30, I-35, I-20, the LBJ freeway . . . In other words, you're going to be limited to a few major highways.

Learning is that way. No matter what the subject matter may be, a person gets to it by a few major routes. Some learners can get there on any of four or five routes. ADD people have only one or two routes. If the educational institution doesn't use those particular routes, the subject matter doesn't enter. And if they are not the routes most of the class uses, the educator probably won't go that way.

There are, however, some tricks the adult or near-adult ADD scholar can use to get ahead. They work both in a formal education setting—they are what successfully got me through my PhD program—and they work well also in informal learning situations.

Informal learning situations hit us not just during the school years but throughout life. Perhaps you move to a new state and have to take the driver's test. You're going to make a presentation as part of your job. You get a home computer, or a new computer at work. You ought to bone up on Canasta rules because the guests who will arrive tonight love Canasta. You get a CD player and have to figure out from the instructions how to operate it. Learning and relearning never end.

As you read here of some aids that promote learning, keep in mind that they also promote productivity in the workplace. I venture to say they can make the difference between doing well in a job and getting fired.

When Learning and Study Don't Come Easily

My fourth grade teacher had this poster titled, "How to Study." It was old when *I* went to school; boys with fifties crew cuts, dressed in slacks and ironed shirts, and girls with their bangs trimmed way up high must have read and demonstrated the precepts listed there.

The poster pictured a quiet, lethargic-looking kid sitting up straight in his wooden chair at his study desk. His feet were flat on the floor. Labels and arrows pointed out that his light was bright, placed a prescribed distance from his work surface, and shining over his left shoulder. His book was a prescribed number of inches away from his eyes (not too close; you don't want to accidentally grow up cross-eyed, the way your parents promised you would if you got too close to what you were reading). He kept his paper and pencils all neatly arrayed where he could reach them easily.

In another picture, a girl sat primly in an upholstered chair that was just exactly her size. (Did they get her a new easy chair every time she grew six inches?) She was not listening to the radio—that was emphasized—and the TV was off. Even the dog beside her recognized a student when he saw one and curled up asleep at her feet instead of bugging her to pet him, let him out, and give him a dog treat, the way my dog always did.

In a third image, a revoltingly wholesome kid was wolfing down a breakfast that would keep a sumo wrestler sated, the idea being that if you ate a lot in the morning you'd do better in school.

There were two other pictures, but I don't remember what they were. I couldn't get over how devoid of reality those three were. Like most educators, my fourth grade teacher was certain that what works for successful students will work for everybody else as well. It took me years—years!—to realize that right-brain ADD kids cannot function in the kind of study environment that poster promoted. This is not a matter of will or preference. They simply cannot.

ADD adults and kids, rather than trying to emulate the left brainers, must discover and exploit their own best ways of learning. They must arrange their best study environment and their best techniques. They must figure out how to complete outside work—homework or outside study in a job. And nothing they come up with will be ways that left brainers claim are "right." But your ways are right—right-brained!

For example, the environment conducive to fruitful study differs greatly for different people.

THE LEARNING ENVIRONMENT

So what kind of learning environment works? Let's say that you have to study to take a driver's test. You have your regular license, but now you want a school bus license or a motorcycle endorsement. You have received material to study.

Keep in mind that studying is not simply sitting at a desk. Many people equate sitting there looking studious with actually accomplishing something. No way. Studying is absorbing information. Any way you can absorb the information is a good way.

You may have a family or a marriage that combines a left brainer and a right brainer. They will require distinctly different environments in order to absorb material. So the comments here may apply in part to several people or very much to one person. In most cases, the non-ADD adult can take the lead in establishing the right environment. Set up an area. Ask the ADD adult how this works, how that works. Two heads working on this situation will get much further quicker than would one.

Light.

Left brainers tend to prefer bright, direct light shining on the material. Right brainers and other ADD students need soft, diffuse light. It can come from anywhere, but preferably not overhead.

Surroundings.

Lefties appreciate quiet. They're the people who do great in a cubicle at the library, over in the Classical Languages section where nobody goes. Television or the radio is very distracting to a lefty. In a particularly distracting environment, such as a fraternity house common area, some lefties profit from soft instrumental music. Words distract; orchestrations serve well as white noise—non-distracting background sounds that drown out other sounds that may divert your attention.

Some righties need white noise in the background. It can really be noise, too. The idea is to drown out distractions. Others need absolute quiet. If I'm studying Scripture, I need no distraction whatsoever—no motion, no noise, no bright colors. If I am trying to listen to a lecturer, noises around me can be extremely distracting—other people whispering, feet shuffling, clothes rustling, papers rattling. And yet that kind of noise does not interfere with other tasks that do not involve hearing. Because white noise is so much a personal thing, varying from individual to individual, you can only experiment until you find what's good for you.

Is television distracting? It might be, depending on what's on. Television has a sort of perverse magnetism that can draw you into it. With its quick cuts and constant change of scene, television is just made for the short attention span which the ADD student is trying to offset. You have to pick and choose the subject and nature of the white noise. That comes by individual trial and error, and television is probably an error. The object is to mask out the movements and distractions that the left brained person would not even notice. Basically, what is white noise to them might provide a major distraction for you.

Posture.

Some left brainers, I've learned, actually can sit up straight at a desk like that kid in the poster and get something done. Not right brainers. In fact, our favorite study position is sprawled out on the floor. When you're already on the floor, you can't drop your pencil very far. Everything can be spread out around you, so that things don't get buried in piles of material. The physical positioning of your body, the sprawl, lends itself to relaxed thinking.

Relaxation is important. ADD students find intensity distracting all by itself. When an ADD student feels anxious, what little attention he could normally muster goes right over the veranda rail.

For formal study occasions, we might drape ourselves all over a chair—one leg hooked over the arm, our backs curved weirdly . . . whatever works.

Whatever works. That's the key.

Beware of a trap. So many times, the non-ADD adult assumes that if a particular study method worked for her, it's the best method for the spouse or kid. Let's say you need quiet in order to concentrate; therefore, you reason, your son had better not be playing the radio while he's trying to read sociology. Your husband shouldn't be listening to the CD player while working on driver's license certification. But your way may not be the best way at all for them. Don't be surprised if your child or mate needs an opposite approach to study. Encourage it! Don't waste you time saying, "Well, when I wanted to study, I'd . . ." That was you. This is different.

Whatever works.

A second consideration in addition to environment is the use of study techniques. Again, everyone is different. I mean everyone. There is a lot the ADD adult can do, in the classroom and on his own, to improve learning. Most ADD adults don't realize it, though. Let me show you techniques that I have found. Pass them on to the ADD mate and encourage him to give them a try.

A word of pleading, here. Attitude is everything. The non-ADD mate who takes the tone of, "You poor dumb bunny, let me, the smart one, help you out of your morass of stupidity," will do nothing of value for the ADD spouse. The quotation overstates the position, of course; no non-ADD mate would actually say that out loud. But you'd be surprised how many feel that way. And the feeling gets communicated whether they intend it or not. That attitude will drive a wedge between spouses, the very thing you do not want.

What can you say that demonstrates a good attitude? "I was reading this book, and Rick Fowler recommends such and so. I encourage you to try it. It worked for him; maybe it can work for you. If there's any way I can help, let me know."

See the difference? Here are the study and learning techniques I found very useful in college. They can be applied far beyond higher education, to any of life's situations where learning in a hurry is required. The ADD adult can use them when learning new skills or a new job or use them in continuing-ed courses and fun stuff down at the Senior Center, such as learning watercolor techniques or ceramics. The sky's the limit.

In all these, the non-ADD spouse must be aware of what the ADD mate is trying to do and how he is trying to do it. And most of all, the non-ADD spouse must facilitate these methods. That's a fancy word for helping to make them happen.

Study Techniques

When was the last time you learned something new through your sense of touch? Babies do it all the time. Small children learn by means of all their senses in the beginning. Sight and sound, taste and smell, touch in its various dimensions all give the child a window on the world. An adult, who knows all about cats, strokes a cat. The small child, by stroking, experiences it.

By about age eight or nine, most kids no longer depend upon taste, smell, and touch so much anymore. A big kid rarely sticks something in the mouth to test it. Touching interesting things is no longer so compelling. A few children—we declare them gifted—retain the ability to learn by more than one means. We call that multisensory learning. These students can take it any way it is presented.

The ADD student, child or adult, has more limited channels, and all too frequently they are not the ones the school uses. Routinely, universities and other schools award 10 percent of their students A's and 10 percent F's. Twenty percent "earn" B's and 20 percent D's. Forty percent receive C's. There's that old bell curve again. When students have trouble learning by the normal channels, they most conveniently supply the failing curve of the bell, and they don't have to be messed with.

If that sounds cruel and heartless on the school's part, consider its position. If every pupil gets good grades, the school's accreditation—not to mention credibility—is questioned. A certain percentage of students are expected to do poorly; that's the prevailing philosophy. And the fact of life in ninety percent of our classrooms, public or private, is that there simply is not enough time to encourage children who cannot learn by "normal" means. It's not humanly possible.

That leaves ADD kids and adults to sink or swim on their own. They need special techniques. Here are some strategies that should help the ADD student survive.

Identify the way you learn.

Here's a concept that will serve every person well no matter how old you are, no matter whether you are ADD or not. Figure out what channels you normally use and the ones you use best. By analogy, figure out which is the best interstate for you to drive on to get into Dallas. You could be a visual learner, a tactile learner, or an auditory learner.

Visual learners generally find reading pretty easy. They learn to read well and early, and they enjoy reading. Put a poster on the wall, and the visual learner studies it and notices its visual elements. This kid or adult has a pretty good eye for estimating distances, sizes, and other spatial information. She does well with maps and diagrams. Visual learners generally don't have much use for being read to. Faced with a choice between a book and a cassette tape or video, they'll take the book.

Auditory learners can talk up a storm, but they tend to have trouble learning to read. Reading may well be painful for them—not in a physical sense but psychologically. It's hard work and they don't like it, but they don't know why. The reason is that reading is visual and they are not. They talk a lot, ask a lot, and in the very process of talking and listening are learning. They prefer books on tape to books in print. They love tapes, in fact. They'll call you up, but don't expect a letter.

Tactile learners have to manipulate and touch what they are learning. To them, hands-on actually means *hands on*. These people really do place a claim on knowledge by touching it. They make excellent cooks and skilled craftsmen. Special ed systems are just now starting to cater to tactile learners. Math lends itself best to their needs. Brightly colored beads, sticks, and bars make the basic math functions simple for tactile learners to comprehend as they physically manipulate the elements to add, subtract, etc. Solid geometry is a snap; you have those three-dimensional shapes to play with.

And then there are, on top of all this, the perennial right-brain/left-brain differences. There really are differences, too, especially in the classroom. Phonics, for example, follow logic; phonics are left-brain. The reading method called "hear-see" or "look-say" is right-brain. Phonics work great with some people; look-say is the only way to get reading across to others.

Promote all your learning channels.

There are some things you can do, however, to improve in all the learning channels. One of the best strategies, and I urge it over and over, is to read to your kids. This activity benefits the adults, ADD and non-ADD, as well as the kids. Reading aloud to children does wonderfully positive things for the reader as well as the listener.

Take the children into your lap, get out that storybook or picture book, and read. Talk about the pictures. Ask questions. Find things. As you read, use exaggerated voice inflections.

When you do that, there is a complex psychological interaction between adult and child in which the child's needs below the conscious level are met. I won't digress into all that here. More to the point at hand, when you use those extreme voice inflections you are honing and encouraging the auditory channels of learning for both the child and yourself. As you talk about the pictures, you are enhancing the visual channels. Your child points to things—that's tactile, hands-on learning.

Analyze how you both, ADD and non-ADD mates, take in information. As you were reading the descriptions above of visual, auditory, and tactile learners, which sounded most comfortable to each of you? Which seemed least attractive? Do you prefer tapes to books? Do you get out and work with your hands a lot because you enjoy it? What is your most comfortable learning style?

Now use it! Let's set up an example here. You and your ADD mate are approaching retirement. Your lives are winding down a little, the kids are nearly grown, and the two of you decide to take an adult education course in Spanish at the local community college. Together you determine that you, the non-ADD mate, are a visual learner and your spouse is an auditory learner. So you tape the sessions and buy the workbook. Your ADD mate plays the tapes over and over as the main study method. You, the visual learner, study by reading the book.

Tactile learning is a little tougher to accommodate. Make

vocabulary and simple grammar flash cards and go through them, holding them in your hands. Pencil in hand, draw a stylized house, for instance. *Una casa.* Discuss it aloud as you draw. Sketch in *el puerto, la ventana*—all the parts of the house—as you say the name of each. If drawing doesn't do it, borrow some blocks from the kids and build a six-block structure, talking about it in Spanish as you work. *Aqui está mi casa. Esto pared tiene una ventana.* Got the idea?

In our hypothetical case here, the two spouses can help each other immensely simply by supporting each other. Respect each other's learning methods; don't try to force what works for you onto your spouse. As both of you grow, that respect will improve.

Know what you want in the classroom.

Do you realize that five years after your high school graduation, you will never see ninety percent of your peers again? At the college level, the percentage of continuing relationships drops still lower. And in adult continuing education, if you didn't go into the class with a person who is a friend, you probably won't come out with a friend. That's important for the ADD student to keep in mind because ADD adults and near-adults tend to worry too much about what others in the class think of them. In short, don't let their negative comments and attitudes affect you. For one thing, you probably won't see much of your classmates after the course is over. You're after an education; don't let them keep you from getting all the learning you can.

There's a phenomenon painfully present in the formal college setting: you're locked in a tussle with everyone else to avoid the bottom of that bell curve. In the eyes of many struggling academic peers, your success becomes their misfortune. If you are in a formal college situation—as are many ADD adults who are just discovering their potential at age twenty-five or thirty or forty—keep this in mind.

What can the non-ADD adult do to help his spouse? As usual, first, understand what the ADD mate's need is—the need to make good contact with the instructor, for example. And then encourage that behavior by whatever means you can find. That's the general directive. The specific steps to take depend solely upon your situation, and no two situations are alike. Can you encourage your mate by explaining what you've learned reading this book? Can you help her study by driving her to class and going over notes? Brainstorm ideas between you.

One technique I suggest for formal college students, ADD adults and all others as well, is to sit at the front of the classroom. There are a couple of reasons why. The biggest, of course, is to minimize the distraction of people around and ahead of you. It's easier to tune out the movement and noise if it's behind you. The second is like unto it: you want your full attention focused on the instructor, and that's easiest to do up front.

Whether or not you are an auditory learner, ask questions during and after class. Do not ask questions for the sake of asking questions. Instructors spot that ploy in a heartbeat. Clarify points that you don't quite understand. Cover any information that you may have accidentally tuned out.

The rule: When in doubt, ask.

And that brings us to another classroom technique: getting to know the teachers and professors. Do it right in the beginning, well in advance of testing. Come to class a little early and learn about the teacher. How many kids does she have? Does he have any hobbies? Do you have anything in common? This isn't flattery. It's marketing! You are out to sell your knowledge and academic achievement, knowing it's not going to show up well through the usual channels. And the teacher/professor is the person you have to sell to. You come out ahead in two ways.

First, the teacher is more likely to give you the benefit of the doubt. For example, suppose your written answer to a question is ambiguous; the teacher isn't clear as to whether you know the right response. The teacher who does not know you from any other student will conclude, "This person is just blowing smoke," and deducts points. The teacher who is familiar with you, on the other hand, will muse, "Knowing how this person thinks and expresses himself, I can pretty safely assume he knows the material." I estimate you can add 10 percent to your grade point average just by knowing the teachers and helping them know you.

Let the teacher know about your test anxiety. Some teachers, burdened with too many duties for too little time, may have to blow you off. But some may also understand and provide alternative ways for you to either take the test or prepare for it. For example, you might ask to take the test orally, with the teacher reading questions and you responding verbally. Or perhaps the teacher can allow you to take the test in a room or cubicle with few distractions. Go for whatever you can and don't be bashful. Your future is at stake, and both you and the instructor will profit.

What if the ADD adult, having followed these suggestions, comes home an hour and a half after the class let out, and gets greeted with, "You left early and got home late. What's going on here, anyway? And besides, I never see you on class nights. You're neglecting me!"

The person who expresses that attitude will sabotage her partner's efforts. The non-ADD adult encouraging the spouse's learning and improvement must weigh every word and criticism. Support comes not so much in lofty deeds as in putting up with the small, everyday sacrifices that the whole family makes to help the ADD adult reach a goal that before now was unthinkable.

Most of what an advanced student must learn comes from outside the classroom. Work consists of text study, lab assignments, and homework. Keeping track of all that and completing it are musts.

Keep track of the work.

Assignments are the bane of the right brainer's educational efforts. When I was in grade school, I couldn't remember assignments long enough to write them down. ADD students get a lot of poor grades and incompletes simply because they don't remember to do the work. And sometimes they suffer because even if they remember to do the work, they forget to turn it in or they lose it.

Here again, the non-ADD mate can be a powerful help. Calendars are second-nature to the non-ADD adult. So sit down with your ADD spouse and help arrange assignments and other deadlines. The ultimate goal of these scheduling sessions is not simply to plan out the work so that the ADD mate can do it. The goal is for the ADD mate to develop the skills to do the planning himself. It's a very subtle difference and very important. It took me a long time by trial and error to figure out how to plan my work. I never asked Jeri, and she didn't know enough about ADD—neither of us did—to volunteer her expertise, to help me develop the skills to do it myself. I could have used her help so much. And she has said many times that she would have been happy to help.

Set up a calendar and mark all due dates. I mean all of them. Make it a big calendar, with plenty of white space in every day's box. Don't put just this month up on the wall by your desk. Put up the next three months, so that your work is literally right before you.

Calendars can help with those huge projects that scare the willies out of you just thinking about them. Term papers! I could write thousands of words when I didn't have to, but assign me a term paper and I froze up. There's a trick to getting long-term projects such as major papers done on time and done well.

Basically, you want to divide your huge assignment into small, manageable bites. Then you give all those small bites due dates and put the bite deadlines on the calendar. It's like driving from Phoenix to New York City. You don't leave Phoenix and drive to New York. You leave Phoenix and drive to Albuquerque. Then you drive to Oklahoma City or maybe even Springfield,

Missouri. And the next day . . . see? You actually make the trip in increments.

Complete only what is scheduled for that day. Then you won't feel pressured or overburdened. When the ADD student perceives that there is no end in sight and toil piles upon toil, we get discouraged. By knowing you have a relatively small task and that once you've completed that task it's over for today, discouragement is minimal.

The non-ADD spouse is the monitor here. The non-ADD spouse, by seeing the overview more clearly, can tell whether the schedule is going to work. The non-ADD mate can see if the individual tasks have been completed. Again, the non-ADD mate cannot simply barge in and rescue the poor, benighted little ADD spouse. The non-ADD mate is a worker and help-meet, not a superior officer. Keep a close check on attitudes.

Let's say the project is a major paper. Pick a day when all your note cards are to be completed. Or schedule the day you will finish the library research. On the next Friday, your rough draft should be done. If Friday rolls around and it's not finished, stay up late until it is.

Meanwhile, your non-ADD mate is sort of keeping an eye on the process. The note cards get done on time, but the rough draft doesn't. The non-ADD mate might be able to offer suggestions for rearranging due dates, suggestions the ADD adult wouldn't notice. On Friday, when the crunch comes, the non-ADD mate supplies the coffee. Or whatever.

And by the next Friday . . . with the components of your project completed one by one, step by step you will not feel so overwhelmed. The non-ADD mate praises and supports and comforts from step to step. With great relief, you eventually find yourself in New York.

I learned to fly that way. When I started taking flight lessons, I had to tell the teacher how to teach me.

He started out, "Here's fifteen hundred pages of material you have to learn."

And I freaked right there. I explained what I needed. He

broke the course down into tiny bites, a page or two at a time. Maybe we'd consume two dozen bites at a lesson, but they were taken in by increments. By the time I soloed, I had those fifteen hundred pages down cold.

Be advised, incidentally, that when most people, ADD or not, complete a major project that's been hanging heavy for some time, they go into free fall for a day or so—unable to get anything constructive done. This recovery period, or refractory period, is normal. Don't browbeat yourself or your mate when it happens.

Homework follows classroom learning as night follows day. You can keep homework in line, again, by playing mind games with yourself.

Complete all home study and homework!

Of course we ADD students ought to mess with our minds; after all, our minds mess with us. Actually, we have to play mind games in order to succeed. And mind games work for us very well because of our competitive nature. If we're not competing with others, we're ready to challenge ourselves.

One way to keep on the track with study is to maintain a distraction sheet. As you sit down to study or write a report or whatever, all sorts of things that you ought to be doing will pop into your head. My dog was a major distractor when I was a kid. About the time I'd settle down to read an assignment, he'd have to go out. Then he'd have to have a treat, and he'd keep pestering me until he got it. Of course, as attention-short as I was, he didn't have to pester much.

While doing homework, keep that distraction sheet close at hand. The moment you think of something that has to be done, instead of doing it, write it down. You'll do it later, when you've studied a minimum of fifteen minutes, half an hour, an hour, or whatever you can manage. You will be surprised how many items on your distraction sheet are no longer urgent or even interesting when you get around to actually doing the stuff.

Don't accept any phone calls during study time, either. Prioritize. The answering machine, the bane of callers everywhere, is a blessing when you are studying.

Here's where the non-ADD spouse can be a great help. Simply covering the distractions, particularly the truly urgent items, is an immense help. If possible, ask your spouse to handle everything, once you sequester yourself for a hardcore learning session. I'm thinking now of a dog whining at the door with his legs crossed. Needs the children have, or think they have. The phone. Heavens to Betsy, the phone!

Reward yourself generously.

Because ADD adults delight in instant gratification, use that particular carrot to keep the ADD adult walking the old treadmill. Generously reward yourself and your mate both for things accomplished.

I've done this many a time. For instance, let's say I have three assignments to prepare. I guesstimate that it's going to take about three hours to do them. My favorite television show comes on at ten. If I get started by seven and stick with it, I can be done in time. I will not allow myself to turn on TV until the assignments are completed. If I don't get them finished by ten, you see, I lose part of my program. My reward for getting them finished is watching TV.

The non-ADD mate is likely the person to introduce this technique, as all the others, to the ADD adult. But this instant reward is not a biggie in the non-ADD adult's life. For the non-ADD mate, a reward six months from now—that diploma or that school bus certification—is sufficient. Too often the non-ADD mate cannot fully grasp that we need something here and now. That means the non-ADD spouse is going to have to voluntarily undertake some major attitude adjustment here.

Also, the non-ADD spouse is the one to oversee the reward process. It is going to be awfully tempting to promise a reward, deliver it, and then cut it short.

Consider this example: An ADD husband loves (and owns) a particular video and hasn't seen it in a couple months. He and his non-ADD wife decide that his reward for fixing the screen door is to sit back and watch his video. He suggested it, and she agreed. He works on the screen door, gets it to work correctly, and pops his video into the player.

Oh, but wait. Not only the screen door but the back porch window needs attention. It sticks. And if he doesn't pull it off and fix it now while the weather is dry, he won't be able to get it open at all. Rain swells it up. Gotta get that window done today; it's going to rain tonight. He can't do that and watch his movie both.

Non-ADD wife steps in. "I know the window needs fixing also, but you did fix the screen door, and a promise to yourself is a promise. Go watch your movie."

See what happened? The ADD husband felt guilty sitting back and relaxing when that other chore seemed pressing. By receiving his wife's support and approval, it was no longer just his selfish interest. She saw the value of his reward also. He could move past the guilt to enjoy his reward in full.

Always capitalize on your full reward. Don't cheat yourself. You have to be able to trust your own word, or pretty soon the technique won't work. And the non-ADD mate is the key with his or her support. So no matter how many additional jobs or assignments loom before me, I sit back and relax and enjoy my reward. I earned it!

Besides, you can use the relaxation because some kinds of stress are particularly deleterious for ADD adults.

Take care to minimize stress.

Stress accentuates any learning difference or difficulty. It makes a strange situation stranger.

For example, the ADD student's mind tends to skip from place to place. This is not daydreaming in the usual sense; it's strictly a physiological quirk. Neurons fire at random and sometimes fail to fire when they ought to. I'll get on an airplane for a three hour flight, intent to do some work en route. Then my mind gets to wandering around, distracted by everything from the guy squashed in next to me to the scenery 35,000 feet straight down. We prepare for landing by returning our seats to their full, upright, and locked position, and I haven't accomplished a thing having to do with work. The time evaporated.

Stress, any stress, multiplies that tendency for the mind to skip around. In fact, it accentuates all ADD tendencies. It may be you are very mildly affected by ADD and under normal circumstances don't notice its effects. Under stress, the symptoms appear. If you didn't have it earlier in life, you won't get it later. But it might be latent, becoming noticeable later when the stresses of life build up.

Stress makes the ADD adult's mind check out. The ADD adult's accumulative memory goes on overload easily, and before you know it, *snap!* The ADD listener misses part of a conversation, or part of a lecture, or the instructions for taking a test, or a stoplight. ("Are you listening?" The answer is, "Yes, but it's not getting through.")

The non-ADD mate can help reduce stress several ways. One is simply by not creating more. Stop and think before you place a criticism or demand where you think it belongs. Ask yourself, "Is this action of mine going to pile on more tension? Can I get around causing that added stress by either phrasing my request some other way or shutting up altogether?"

The other way is for the non-ADD mate to adjust his or her own attitude more to the right brainer's. We have all, ADD and non-ADD adults alike, been taught throughout life that "you gotta do this now! The world will fall apart if you don't succeed right this minute." There's a sort of urgency applied to learning or succeeding in some other way that simply is not really there. Here, the non-ADD mate must make some significant changes in attitude because the left-brain position is, "In order to succeed, you must constantly succeed."

A significant way to minimize stress then is to counter that philosophy. The ADD and non-ADD adult both should remind themselves that there isn't anything about the learning situation that's all that do or die. If you don't succeed now, do it again. If this doesn't work, you now know this doesn't work. So try that.

Even in grade school, ADD kids and others get the message that it's incredibly important to succeed right now. "You'll be a nothing forever if you don't do well with this grade, or test, or project, or year." Schools place so much emphasis on the minor, inconsequential things of the moment that kids miss the fun of being a kid. So do grown-ups. And all that piles on stress.

Exercise reduces stress, so I exercise as much as possible. Deep breathing exercises also help relieve stress. They're especially good just prior to heavy-stress tasks such as exams and big assignments or presentations.

Tests and exams. Talk about stress! There are, however, a suite of techniques ADD adults (non-ADD people, too) can use to minimize test anxiety and score well.

Taking Tests and Exams

"Oh, by the way, we have a test tomorrow . . ."

Fear grips the heart and robs the breath. Some react by freezing like a bunny on the interstate when they hear the dreaded T word.

The major reason ADD students panic is insecurity, a fear of the unknown. Another reason is that old familiar problem, control concerns. No way are you in control when a test is coming at you; you cannot govern how you will do or even what will be on it. And pop quizzes? To an ADD student, a pop quiz packs the pop of a twelve gauge shotgun!

A third reason ADD students fear tests—the technical term, incidentally, is test anxiety—is that tests are geared to left-brain skills such as rote memorization and organization of thought and are therefore alien to an ADD student.

Getting low grades damages a student's concentration. That's been shown. When the student had minimal concentration ability to start with, the very act of getting low grades can further damage concentration and lead to still more low grades—and down and down it spirals. The fear of this downward spiral can be a major block against performing well in tests.

Related to that is the point, all too often true, that grades determine self-esteem. It should never be true, but it almost always is. A lot of parents signal to the kids (often not at a conscious, verbal level) that their worth depends on getting that A, earning that B.

Tests, whether they be for your graduate degree or your driver's license, do not have to scuttle the ship of happiness. Here's how to get through them with your hull intact. A lot you do in advance, but there are a few tricks to try at the time of the test as well. Incidentally, if you wait until the last minute you'll shoot yourself in the foot for sure. ADD adults can't handle the stress of cramming. Taking tests well requires advance work.

Let's set up a hypothetical situation here. Again, I'll make the ADD spouse a male, for no particular reason. He's forty-five, been with his company almost twenty years. His job as a die cutter is being phased out, and he's supposed to go down to Phoenix for three months of intensive training for a new job. In the new work he will handle a computer that cuts the dies.

The test? At the close of the course, he will be called upon not only to operate the computer/robot/die cutter but also to trouble-shoot problems the instructors will invent. If he doesn't pass, he's laid off and they bring in someone younger, smarter. That's a pretty stiff grade for a test. Lots of pressure. The company hands him a plane ticket to Phoenix and a training manual that might as well be written in Sanskrit and wishes him luck.

What's a guy to do?

Set up your support.

The first thing this guy does is buy his non-ADD wife a ticket to Phoenix also. He's going to need help with this. Reliable help. She can get him through it.

An adult college student—which is what I was—needs the help just as much as this man does, but the college student's wife will probably be dividing her time between him and the kids. The ADD adult in that situation must recognize that the non-ADD spouse has only twenty-four hours in a day. He (or she, of course) may have to do without or accept only desultory help. You do what you can do.

Know what you're supposed to learn.

If you are in a formal classroom situation, at the very first of the semester or quarter, query your instructor. Ask something along the lines of, "I'm studying X, Y, and Z. Am I on the right track?" Observe the instructor's responses carefully. You want to know what to expect—there's that old fear of surprises issue again in new garments. But it's not an unreasonable request whether you're right-brained or not.

Our sample gentleman, the one training in Phoenix, not only discusses with his instructors what he's supposed to learn in these next three months, he talks about it with his wife. She should know what he has to learn also. She may well have insights into how he can go about learning it. She will help with scheduling the material in increments. She has to know what they're working with.

Compile and condense notes.

This is not exactly test preparation; it's learning; but it's test preparation as well in the most important sense. Every day, take notes. Pay particular attention to anything written on the board. This is mostly, of course, for the college student who sits in a lecture hall three or four hours a week per course. If you are an auditory learner, tape your classes; but take written notes as well. You can thumb through written notes a lot easier than you can thumb through a tape to find a particular piece of information. But the tape is useful, too; it gets every word and nuance.

Now, here's where the die cutter parts company with others. He copies his notes, rewriting, adding other things he's picked up. *He does this every class day.* He'd lose elements if he did not. The rewrite will cement facts in his mind as nothing else can.

The wife helps out by reading his notes aloud to him and drilling him on the contents. You see, he's an auditory learner, and when they talk it back and forth, he really gets the material. Just taping the lecture notes was all right, but this verbal give-and-take aids immensely.

It's a sort of inside-out twist on the basic theme of, "Honey, are you listening?" Now the ADD partner is listening for purposes of self-interest. And can the non-ADD mate tell when he's tuning out? You bet! She asks him questions now and then on what they just talked about.

As if the textbook were a lecturer, the die cutter takes notes from it as well. Highlighting is nice, but taking notes is better. Again, he and his wife give the notes an auditory once-over.

This technique works for formal class work as well. The week before a major test, condense all your lecture notes down to fit on a single sheet of paper. Write small. Summarize. Squeeze. Eliminate margins. Get it on there. Now condense the textbook notes you made down to one page. Read the text again, or scan it.

Do you see the mind game you're playing with yourself? Twenty pages of notes is daunting. One page you can handle. "These two pages? That's all? Piece of cake!"

Somewhere down inside, your mind knows it's being flummoxed, but it lets you get away with it. Perhaps instead of a paragraph in the original notes, you're left with a few words. Those few-word reminders are enough to call up the whole. Remember that ADD students can put it all in; it's retrieving it again that causes the problems. You know the material. This one page of terse, abbreviated notes helps you bring back what you know.

These study methods work very well for task completion in other areas of life as well. Just as you take what you learned in school out into real life, you can take these methods also.

You will be called upon to make a presentation of some sort. Maybe it happens often to you. Trim your notes down to one page. It works great for anything from introducing the speaker at your service club meeting to presenting a whole new accounting system to your company president. I am constantly intrigued by how much of one aspect of life spills over into all the others.

The die cutter didn't get tests during the course the way college students would, so he has no idea whether he's absorbing what he needs. His wife can help. She can review the written material; she reads faster than he and retains more. Does he know what's in the book?

Study without cramming.

To study for a formal test specifically, clear your desk of every distraction. Lay those two pages of notes out before you and only those two pages. Use them to study, to remind yourself what you know.

Frankly, the instructor who says, "Test Friday. Be ready!" isn't teaching anyone in the class study skills. Sure, now you know it's coming, but what do you *do?* A really good teacher, and I've had a few, teaches study skills by showing you the goal—that is, where the end is—and then gives the students an increment each day for reaching that goal.

Don't try to cram the day of your exam. That works for some people, but not for ADD folks. Let your system calm down so that your anxiety level is low.

In fact, just before you walk into a test, do a few deep-breathing exercises. Draw in as much air as you'll hold, keep it in there a moment, and let it out slowly. It helps you relax, it oxygenates your brain, and it provides an excellent pause in which to pray for God's wisdom and help.

And when you take the test . . .

When you go in to the test, before you even look at the questions, immediately turn the paper over and on the back jot down dates, names, and figures that your brain might stumble on later. Take a moment or two to put them down in black and white before you have to think of them officially, so to speak. Now turn the paper back over and begin the test.

Skim the questions and answer the ones you're sure about first. Next answer the ones you can give a pretty good guess. Finally, take a wild shot at those you may not know. Don't leave any question unanswered. People debate the relative advantages and percentages between whether you guess cold or leave it blank, but for your psychological good, fill in every item. The ADD adult has trouble completing a project. This is one you want completed.

When the test is returned after grading, discuss questionable items with the instructor. This does two things. For one, it tells the teacher (we hope) that you actually know more than what that test measured. You may or may not get an improvement on your grade, but you just might get the benefit of the doubt next time. Second, if the teacher is aware that you are interested and will debate your view in a positive—not confrontational—way, he or she may think twice about marking you wrong the next time, especially on a subjective question.

Our die cutter will take only one test, and that at the very end. All or nothing. Cramming won't work for him either. So his wife supports him in several different ways. For one, she helps him with preparation, as we have noted above. His cramming, in essence, begins weeks before the end. She helps him learn all the little pieces of information that, when taken together, give him competence in his brand new skill. (He *hates* computers; he's learned that much so far.)

Also, she helps him reduce stress, particularly as test time approaches. They drive out into the desert near Red Mountain, to the state park. They take a two-day trip to the Grand Canyon.

They go downtown to the art museum to look at the wonderful Thorne rooms. They discuss (more verbal interaction) how they would build a room like these. Could he use his die-cutting skills to reproduce that amazing King Louis XIV table? Not only is she helping him find and use stress-relievers, she's helping him integrate his learning into his daily life and dreams.

Finally, she handles distractions, especially toward the end. No one talks to him without going through her. He's busy. She'll handle your phone call.

And she will help by adjusting her attitude, forsaking "You *must* succeed or else!" which is essentially the world's attitude, in favor of a more fitting attitude. "Let's ask God's blessing and see what happens with this."

Attitude is so important to the ADD adult in a learning situation!

The ADD student would do well to look at the test not as a test but as a game. Here's where you mess with your own mind big time. You're pitting your skills against the test compiler's. That compiler, almost certainly some left-brain whiz, has stacked the test against you because it does not reflect the way you think and learn. Your mission, should you choose to accept it, is to thwart the compiler's left-brain slant and, in the process of thwarting him, shine.

In fact, one of the best mind games you can play with yourself is to put the whole subject of study and learning into an ADD student's perspective.

Putting Study in Perspective

Here we have little Ricky Fowler, age nine or ten, and he's having a terrible time with his attention deficit. So what do we tell him? "You have to do well in school, or twenty years down the road you won't be able to hold down a good-paying job."

Here's little Ricky at age seventeen, having been sternly advised never ever to attempt going to college. There are a couple of subjects he simply cannot master to save his life. He's doing fine in part of his studies, woefully in others. So what do we tell him? "You're going to have to have a better college grade point average than that to get anywhere, Bucko." This is followed by, or preceded by, "Everybody has to take these prerequisites, and you don't seem to be doing too well in them."

And then some joker comes up to Rick the adult, still plagued by living an ADD life in a left-brain world, and says, "Ah, it's not so hard. Anybody, ADD or not, can make it if they just apply themselves and study."

You want to shoot the bozo.

The whole point is, no matter how hard the ADD individual "applies" himself, success does not come easily or automatically. It's probably the one lesson the non-ADD mate finds hardest to absorb. Applying by itself doesn't cut it. Using unorthodox methods just might.

By getting creative, the ADD adult or near-adult can avoid jumping through all the hoops some people think you ought to. When I was considering college, my high school GPA was 2.2. No way does a college welcome 2.2 students. A professor suggested I enter as a non-degree candidate. In that student classification, GPA doesn't matter. I took some courses apart from the prerequisites. My determination was there, but I had to learn the little tricks of successful learning, and that took practice. Lo and behold, I started making high B's and A's, and I was on my way.

What was Jeri doing as I worked my way through college the long and circuitous route? Being patient. It's what the non-ADD adult has to do, and it doesn't come easy. Left brainers want to whip through the learning situation, whatever it is, and go on to the next thing. We ADD adults may have to dawdle along a little slower. There are other ways around problems also.

A guy I know who has some real learning difficulties flunked his required math course for the third time. Without that course he couldn't get the engineering degree he wanted, and three times and you're out. He figured he was out of options and was ready to quit.

"No, no, no!" said I. "Wait." We went through the college catalog together. Here was an option of a business degree with an engineering emphasis. He'd have to pick up several business courses, but he didn't need that bugger math course that was doing him in. He earned the business degree, and with all his engineering electives, he got a great job—in the engineering field!

Another example: an ADD college student is having trouble getting certain required courses out of the way. It might take a little longer, but there are ways to get around that barrier. For instance, let's say college student RF, slaving away at University A, has trouble getting good grades in foreign languages. Certain foreign languages are required of every University A graduate. RF studies the college catalog to learn what courses are transferable. Then RF takes his foreign language courses at school B, sometimes repeating them, until he earns pretty good grades in the required courses. Then he transfers that grade over to University A. He thereby preserves his grade point average at A, where the degree is coming from.

Is that cheating? Absolutely not. How do ADD students come up with schemes like that? Actually, it's not hard. Remember that ADD people tend to think globally, coming up with nonlinear, and therefore unusual, solutions to problems. If you have a question about a proposed technique or sideways move, talk to a high school or college guidance counselor or to the administrative office about feasibility. Beware, however, of the prevailing mind-set, "You can't do that because it's never been done that way." Make sure it won't work; don't take a negative response at face value.

And the non-ADD mate? Do, do, do try not to be the negative response. No ADD adult needs to hear, "It's never been done. It won't work!" from the person nearest and dearest to him. Jeri, bless her, got with my sometimes weird programs and helped me. She sometimes altered my suggestions into something more manageable or affordable, as when she cancelled my plan to sell the house and instead launched me on a remodeling project (which I loved, once I got into it).

Do you see what a delicate balance of give-and-take is required here? The ADD adult must respect the mate's opinion, and the non-ADD mate must avoid being an instant wet blanket.

But long before college, parents must let their kids pursue their own interests, rather than their parents'. That's not easy. I have a friend in New Mexico, in the logging business. He wants more than anything else in the world for his son to follow in his footsteps, as he followed in his own father's. And his boy, an ADD adolescent entering ADD adulthood, is really good in the woods. He knows the trade. But he doesn't want to do it. He wants to be a diesel mechanic. He keeps his dad's rigs running, and all the neighbors'. He loves it. He feels that logging is not a good career choice anymore, but mechanics is. What a tragedy it will be if his father presses his own dreams so hard that he alienates and estranges his son.

What that boy needs most of all is a young wife who can share his dream. That's really the ultimate need—sharing the dream. It's also true of advanced education, whatever form it may take. Almost all continuing education, adult education, and college is dream-empowerment. During rough times, the not-fully-empowered dream can die so easily. The non-ADD mate can help keep those dreams alive as no one else can, not even parents and trusted friends. It takes time, too.

Grade school is the time to encourage kids' dreams and keep their enthusiasm high. You see, the ADD child may not be able to work out good study techniques until late high school or college, when he or she is striving to succeed academically because of some goal. Believe me! Telling little Ricky Fowler, age nine, to study so that he can make big money in twenty years is useless. Not only can ADD kids not see that far ahead, they can't continue making the sacrifice of blood, sweat, and tears with no validation, and that's what grade school is normally like for them.

So how do you motivate the ADD student if a distant goal won't work? By considering school a game.

When I was a kid, that was the only way I could win. ADD and other learning-different kids, who cannot see the future and don't care about it, quickly adapt to the idea of school as a competitive game. We *love* rough and ready games! And it's not so outlandish a proposal.

Despite what some left-brain folk think, school is not a life-or-death proposition, with the outcome of the next test determining whether the free world will remain safe for democracy. If it's a game in which you can come out ahead most of the time, or even some of the time, your worth is no longer measured by school performance. If you strike out on an exam, you step back up to the plate for the next one. Shucks, pro ball players get on base only about thirty percent of the time.

With an attitude like that, immediately, an awful lot of school anxiety and test anxiety evaporates. We plug along; we try to win; we do anything moral and legal to win. And if our batting average tops five hundred we rejoice.

We either take back roads or canoe up the Trinity River, but by cracky, we get to Dallas.

The die cutter case was hypothetical based upon a friend's actual experience (he wasn't a die cutter; he was something else). Did he pass his test? He did indeed. Six months later he took a pay cut to move over to another division where he could work hands-on with final assembly. Six months after that the final assembly line was automated, and he was right there with his computer expertise, this time as a trainer. He received an in-house service award, for which he gave his wife full credit. When he said, "I could never have done this without her," he was speaking the truth.

This was a guy whose teachers claimed, "The kid will never amount to anything." His wife was the woman of whom acquaintances said, "She's so smart. Why did she ever marry that dolt?"

She married him because she was smart.

Obviously, if they are to succeed, learning situations depend heavily upon organization. Indeed, a lot of life depends upon organization. I'm a real bear about organization—call me obsessive—simply because, left to my natural devices, I am totally chaotic in thinking and living. Other ADD adults and I have developed ways of organizing life. Often the non-ADD mate can contribute powerfully, not so much by doing things for the ADD adult as by providing balance. Let's look at how to turn your chaotic life into an ordered one.

FIVE

ADDept Organization

Jeri speaks:
Three of the most dreaded words in parenthood are "Some assembly required." We were going to put together a child's tricycle. It came in a box. It couldn't be that hard, right? After all, we saw kids riding around on trikes all the time. We opened it up and spread all the pieces around, and Rick panicked.

He simply panicked. I figured we were in trouble, if a man with some mechanical ability turns white looking at a project. I didn't know what to do, so when all else fails you follow the directions. I did step 1. Then I did step 2. Rick helped and we got the handlebars on right.

About step 10 we had to put the back wheels on with a pal nut driver. We had screwdrivers and wrenches and hammers in the house, but no pal nut driver. So we used a sewing thread spool and a tack hammer. Worked fine.

At the end, around step 25 or so, there sat the brand new

trike, and all those loose parts were used up except for one weird little metal part left over. It looked kind of like a half-inch wide derby hat. So we looked it up on the back page of the instructions where each part was pictured. It was the pal nut driver.

Rick speaks:
We were walking along a ridge north of Dallas one day. Gorgeous afternoon. Blue sky, golden late-season grass rippling in the breeze, clumps of brush scattered across the slope. Suddenly a covey of quail burst out right in front of us. *Right* in front of us. Fluffy feather-balls exploded up and out in all directions. One whirred past my ear. As they scattered out across the slope, they set their wings and went to ground just beyond the next clump of brush or the ridge top or the deep grass. They disappeared; if they hadn't squirted up in front of me I'd never have suspected they were anywhere around.

An ADD adult's thoughts are just like that. They explode out of nowhere, scatter, and disappear. We can't control them; we can't keep track of them. They can be so obvious you can't miss them, and moments later they disappear.

And yet, I've not often seen something quite as beautiful and remarkable as that covey of quail. Despite the frantic nature of their exit, they were so well coordinated one with another. And of course, the birds themselves are charming and beautiful.

Unfortunately, when your mind behaves like that covey, getting through life can be frustrating. Using little tricks to keep track of the quail can make all the difference.

The Balancing Act of Organization

Something like this conversation took place in my office during a counseling session. See how many phrases ring a bell for you.

TED: I don't know why we're even trying this. I can't see that talking about our problems is going to do anything to solve them. I'm only here because Sue asked me to come.

SUE: Well, something's going to have to happen here. I've been trying my best to make our marriage work, and Ted just doesn't give a hang.

TED: I do too! I do the best I can.

SUE: What about last night? I called you just before you left your office and asked you to pick up some milk. We were out and Meg wasn't up from her nap yet. I couldn't go, or I would have, believe me. You promised! And you came home without it. You weren't listening a bit. You don't even care enough to get milk for your babies!

TED: I do too care! I wrote it down before you even got off the phone. (A sheepish pause.) But then I forgot the note.

SUE: So write it on your hand or something. I'm sick and tired of keeping track of every single detail in life while you abandon your responsibility completely.

TED: (Acidly.) I'm very, very sorry I'm not the mild-mannered robot you think I ought to be.

Before the conversation deteriorated any farther into sarcasm and diatribe, I stepped in and led it off in other directions.

You've seen arguments like this one a million times. One spouse is super-organized and the other can't find a T-shirt in a drawer. Polarized. If marriage were a seesaw (which, figuratively, it is), both partners would be scooted way back on the edge of their seats, getting as much leverage as possible. And that is exactly it. They both sense that if one spouse were too moderate, moving closer to the center fulcrum of the teeter-totter, the other out there on the tip end would gain all the advantage. Remember that for an ADD mate, control looms very large in life.

But if someone sits midway up the board and the other sits out at the end, the teeter doesn't totter. It is also the natural bent of human beings to be on the move, literally and figuratively—our species is the most nomadic of creatures. The other partner has to scoot in toward the middle to get the seesaw moving again. And that, too, parallels relationships.

In the case of Ted and Sue and the forgotten milk, she had moved out to the far end of the responsibility seesaw. She called him at the optimal time to remind him; in short, she did everything in her power to make him responsible. She would have taken over the whole ball of wax and gotten the milk herself if the baby hadn't been asleep.

And Ted? He was out at his end of the responsibility teeter-totter, being as irresponsible as possible. He not only forgot the milk, he forgot the note.

Keeping the seesaw in mind, let's explore the ways an ADD spouse and mate can balance each other well without letting life dissolve into frustration and acrimony. We'll look at ways the ADD spouse can make life smoother through better organization, and then we'll discuss ways the ADD person's mate can adjust to improve comfort.

The ADD Adult's Organization

You should see my office. Everything I know, and I mean everything, is on a piece of paper somewhere in my office.

"This is not organization," complained an acquaintance as she looked around in dismay. "This is neotomosis."

Neotomosis? Later I learned that *neotoma* is the scientific name for pack rat. Very funny.

All that material in my office is not just things of interest squirreled away for someday. You see, like most ADD adults, I have a lot of information tucked away in my brain, but I have trouble accessing it. I can't pull out the data I need from memory when I need it. By stashing everything in a fairly organized manner in my office, I know where it's written down. I can get to it when I want it.

And that is a clue for how an ADD adult can start getting not only organized but heavier—that is, carrying more weight on the seesaw of responsibility.

WRITE IT DOWN

Just about everything that goes on in my brain goes down on paper. An ADD adult has to work that way. The ADD adult's mate has to recognize that information is not as freely accessible to recollection in the ADD adult as it is in most people, and all those notes and stacks of information are vitally necessary.

I even use a pencil when I'm thinking. As I write down thoughts and arrange them, I can organize my thinking better. Because ADD adults aren't all that good at linear thinking, we have to be able to see it lined out, so to speak.

If you commit your thinking to paper, try making use of spatial arrangement. Let's use a simple but ludicrous example. I'm a mouse wanting to figure out how to put a bell on the cat. I write the problem out not in a straight line but in a little blob in the middle of a big sheet of paper. "Bell on cat." How can such a bell be attached? In clustered blobs around the periphery of the paper I write down any ideas on how to get it to stay on. Velcro. Chewing gum. A collar. A rubber band, the way they make bows stay in poodles' hair. Then I consider who might do it. Me. The cat's mistress (fat chance of that!). The cat himself. Fate.

Notice that I did not just *think* my original question. I wrote it down in the center of the page. That is so I will keep my mind on the problem. Otherwise, my thoughts are likely to skip off in other directions and I'll forget the original problem. By placing it in the middle, I keep it central to my thinking. Position means a lot.

As my thought process continues, I might draw lines from one feasible element to another. Get the mistress to put a collar on the cat; line from there to there. In the end, the paper is arranged globally, the way I think, not linearly. I can see a broad variety of elements at one glance. I have arranged my thinking on paper approximately the way it goes on in my particular mind. Other people would arrange their thinking in other patterns reflecting their uniqueness.

For an ADD adult, writing is the key to memory.

That goes for short-term memory also. I always have a notebook and pencil on me. I carry a little cassette recorder on my belt, too. I got a leather company to build me a custom holster for it so I won't lose it. When I'm out on the road or on a trip, the minute I think of something, I say it onto a tape. This is especially helpful when I'm driving because it's dangerous to whip out a paper and pencil on the interstate.

BUILD A WORK SYSTEM

My work day would be chaotic if I didn't build some sort of external system for keeping the work flowing. For example, I work with files a lot. In fact, I try to organize everything I do into files. Files are small, comfortable units—just my style. In the morning, I stack all the files I anticipate using that day to my right. Finished work and no-longer-needed files go to the left. I may leave a file in the middle of my desk overnight to cue me as to what I must do the next morning first thing.

An acquaintance exclaimed, "Oh, you're so organized!"

It's all on the outside, where it shows. I'm organized externally because I have to be.

You may or may not use files. You may or may not have a work situation that can be converted to a system of files. No matter. Your work load can be arranged somehow. Perhaps little slips of paper will do it. Several companies offer a system in which you write your task or sub-task on a color-coded square card and slip it into a sleeve, key words sticking out, in a ring binder. You might have twelve sleeves on a binder sheet, or twenty. Each holds part of a project you're working on, or a person you should call or write—whatever. It's a great system.

Devise your own such system if you wish. Make it simple; complex systems get abandoned quickly because they take too much time. Customize it so it's yours alone. Don't use mine. Let mine give you ideas for your own. Keep in mind also that organization requires that you have a place for everything.

Have a Place for Everything

Not just information flow suffers because of the ADD spouse's special approach to organization—or lack of it. Our material possessions suffer as well.

The ADD adult *must* put away tools immediately, or they're lost in the chaos. The ADD adult *must* hang up clothes, shelve books, and put pens and other paraphernalia in an assigned place. Of course, the non-ADD spouse must be equally careful to return items to their assigned place.

Some years ago I read a short celebrity squib that I just love. According to the piece, Phil Donahue asked his wife, Marlo Thomas, "Where are my shoes?" And she retorted, "Where are *my* shoes?" The implication: "It is not my job to look after your possessions." To each his own.

There's that seesaw again. The more a non-ADD mate cleans up after the spouse, putting things away, picking up, the more the ADD partner needs the service. This is not laziness, exactly. The ADD mate quickly learns to depend upon the spouse to find what's been carelessly lost, to pick up what's been cast down. Unfortunately, because the ADD mate is not the one putting things back, that person is constantly less likely to re-member where the objects are supposed to be because there's been no memory reinforcement. The moment the non-ADD mate is out of the picture—out of town, visiting, working differ-ent hours—the ADD spouse is at a total loss in the kitchen, the den, the bathroom, the garage. In short, the non-ADD mate does the spouse no favors by picking up and keeping track.

If the seesaw has slipped out of balance at your house, now's the time to come to agreement. The ADD person, lousy memory or not, is responsible for his or her own things.

But what about long-term memory? I may not be in my office when I need some information that's dutifully recorded on a piece of paper there. Or I'll meet someone I know that I know and not recall the name. (Incidentally, it's been a long, hard haul, but I've finally learned not to feel guilty about not remembering names.) Here's where Jeri is a wonderful help. Although the ADD adult must not toss organization off onto the non-ADD mate, there are times when the non-ADD mate can balance out what the ADD spouse needs. There is a time to ask for help.

Accept Help

Poor Jeri. At first, she thought that she somehow embarrassed me because I wasn't introducing her to my friends. That couldn't be farther from the truth! Still, it wasn't until she came to understand about ADD that she realized what was really happening and we worked out a game plan. Now if I fail to introduce her, she introduces herself and I act as though I thought she already knew the other person. It works every time. That's because it's true, as likely as not. I can't remember names and faces and who knows whom and all that.

She's not always available, of course, but when she is, she graciously fills in what I lack. Jeri, who is very good at names and faces, will take the initiative in a meeting or conversation. She'll say the person's name aloud, cuing me. When we're introduced to people, she'll use their name every now and then where I can pick it up. Following casual conversations, as at a party or dinner, she'll review for me what was said while I write it down. I cannot remember the tenor of conversations until I'm reminded, but she can keep it straight. As to other details and facts, she can access her memory like nobody's business. I can ask her, and she'll give me the information faster than I could find it in my neotomatic office.

I have a friend—actually the friend of a friend—who will phone his wife and ask, "How do you spell *disintegration?*"

"D-I-S-I-N-T-E-G-R-A-T-I-O-N."

"Thank you. I love you." He hangs up.

One of the many reasons he loves her is that she's a superb speller, and he can barely spell his own name.

There are aspects of organization that you can borrow from study methods. One is the process of dividing daunting tasks into manageable pieces.

Live Life in Small Increments

I could have subtitled this section "Live life in manageable chunks."

When something big and chaotic comes up, I can't manage it well. Like a disassembled tricycle, a pile of pieces looks hopeless and instantly discouraging. I'm not alone. A friend tells of her sister purchasing a dollhouse several years ago. (She informs me that dollhouses are not for children; properly done, they're adult toys.) The sister opened the carton and here were hundreds and hundreds of bits of wood. Individual shingles. Wooden strips instead of assembled windows. The sister bought my friend an airplane ticket and flew her a thousand miles to come put the dollhouse together for her.

More so than most people, ADD adults lose perspective and lose heart when a project looms large. Probably it's because we know only too well that our attention span cannot encompass a complex or lengthy task. When a job like that confronts us, we simply cannot see the solution that seems so obvious to others: start with Step 1.

And yet, I learned to fly a plane one step at a time. You mow the lawn one section at a time. Life is lived in increments, and it's the only way ADD adults can function well.

In this case you're not just playing mind games with yourself, the way you do when you set up rewards. The ADD adult's mind really does work in small increments, one limited thing at a time. You're simply using your mind to its fullest, just as the left brainer memorizes multiplication tables easily and may not need a calculator most of the time.

To avoid friction and acrimony, the non-ADD mate must keep that in mind when assigning tasks. The non-ADD mate who organizes generalized tasks into specific, clearly stated sub-tasks is not only doing the ADD spouse a favor but helping himself as well, for it's the only way the job will be completed satisfactorily.

The non-ADD mate, when requesting that a job be done, is wise to line out the steps verbally, or list them. Break it down. Make sure the request is clear, that it is understood, and that it is made in the form of manageable bites. The non-ADD adult does not always think that way, so it's not easy for him or her.

For instance, "Paint the garage" becomes:

1. Mask the two windows and the glass panels in the door.
2. Scrape the window frames.
3. Hose down all four walls, including the doors.
4. Rent the sprayer.
5. Spray the walls.
6. Clean up the sprayer.
7. Return it.
8. Paint by hand the trim on the windows.
9. Remove the masking.
10. Check each side in turn for missed spots. Touch up.
11. Clean up the brushes.
12. Take paint cans to hazardous materials shed at landfill.
13. Throw away paper, rags, stirring sticks.
14. Scrape any remaining paint off window glass with a razor blade.

Some of the sub-tasks are more fun than others, but they all share the virtue of being short and manageable. They reach a goal.

Like budgets, which are financial goals, I suppose, goals are extremely distasteful to ADD adults. They constrict. They limit. They impose requirements. They channel.

They are also absolutely necessary for good organization.

Develop Goals

When I was a young and carefree lad, the last thing in the world I wanted shaping my life was goals. Live each day as it comes! Step forth and let the Lord guide you! Setting forth a goal was tantamount to digging your own rut. I'd have none of it.

I know better now.

To a person who loves his or her own impulsivity (and Jeri claims that at times my impulsivity is indeed a lot of fun), goals are not chains that bind, even though they may seem to on the surface. Without them, the ADD adult bounces off walls all the way through life. You know, that aimlessness gets boring in itself. Without some aim to strive for, life gets a little monotonous after a while, and you usually don't even know why.

Goals give you something to shoot for, a reason to move forward. They offer purpose. Most important, goals curb impulses that can be detrimental. They give you focus and provide a solid overall organization.

Let's say I make it a goal to buy a house. Now when I'm twenty years old, that's not an attractive goal at all. What do I need with a house? A house ties you down. But there may come a day when I'm not able to travel for one reason or another. That house will be a pretty nice comfort. Besides, I'll be winning the financial game. Yep, another game, and an important, high-stakes one.

You see, there's this struggle between me and the rest of the world over where my money's going to go. When I fritter my money away with nothing to show for it, the world has won the battle. Unless I set goals such as the purchase of a house, the world is going to win the war. With my goal, I win because it keeps me focused on a sound investment.

It's not easy for ADD folks to develop goals and stay in focus. A non-ADD mate can render splendid service here by helping set the goal, then brainstorming with you to find creative ways to meet it.

Goals are not a cure-all that gives your life sudden perfect organization. Sometimes there gets to be too many goals. You have to back off some of them in order to succeed at one of them. Be prepared for that. If my goal is the purchase of a house, the yacht is going to have to wait. If my goal is to get the garage cleaned out by May first, going to Tempe, Arizona to watch spring training may have to go by the board. On the other hand, that garage is such a mess, and going to Tempe is a pretty neat reward for steamrolling the project and completing it in a timely manner. Weigh goals and options.

Goals imply self-discipline. Your degree of self-discipline and your attitude toward it both stem from your upbringing to a great extent. I was raised in a very left-brained world. Frankly, calling it legalistic is not really misrepresenting it. I was taught as much self-discipline as my ADD would permit. It was a painful situation very frequently; those around me would impose standards of discipline that my ADD simply did not allow. But now, in retrospect, I am immensely grateful that they taught me a degree of discipline and self-control. But oh my, didn't I hate it then!

I'm certainly not what most folks would call solidly self-disciplined even now. So I can say with authority that when the ADD mate lacks that self-discipline, he or she must ask help from the mate. A steadying hand can make all the difference.

When discipline perseveres and you meet a goal, that's a pretty heady win. You've won out over your ADD nature to avoid living beyond the moment. You win because you've gained control over yourself, and control is always a tasty morsel for the ego. Your goal, presumably, is a desirable end that will benefit you—another win.

When I first began developing goals, I had to win for me. Now that I've come to appreciate goals, I can win for the sake of my family and for the Lord.

Goals—I've grown to love 'em.

In what specific ways can the non-ADD mate participate in goal-setting? That depends upon the couple, for no two pairs of people are the same. Neither do any two persons interrelate the same ways others do. The above suggestions then are guidelines, not specific instructions. We are so individualistic, it must be thus.

But the ADD adult and non-ADD mate can take a big step further, beyond just helping each other out. They can make the intellectual and emotional adjustments that create a true working harmony between them. Adequate organization can exist for both without that harmony, but really good organization requires it. Otherwise they are working much of the time at cross purposes.

Most non-ADD mates take a certain heady pride in being on top of things with organization, memorized data, facts and figures. Let's face it. They feel superior to us ADD folk. And in that particular regard, they are. Encourage your non-ADD mate in his or her gifts, and rejoice in them.

But you have gifts also, and they deserve both recognition and reward. Another study technique that works splendidly in the workaday world is a reward system.

CREATE REWARDS FOR YOURSELF

Rewards will help keep you on the straight and narrow path of organization. Here's mind-twisting at its best, only it's your own mind. I think up rewards to keep myself going with a project. Let's say I have to mow the lawn and wash the car, and there's a college basketball game at two. I hate mowing the lawn. It's a major bore. Washing the car isn't all that invigorating to me, either. However, it's a small lawn and a compact car. If I start an hour before the game, I can get both projects and a shower done in time for tipoff. Get the lawn done! Get the car washed! Hop in, hop out, dig out a pair of clean jeans, kick back in front of the TV, and enjoy that game! You accomplished your objectives, you completed onerous chores, you've won out over the world yet again. Good for you!

A word of caution about rewarding yourself: keep rewards

commensurate and don't cut them short. For example, a vacation in Hawaii would be a nice reward, but it's not commensurate with mowing the lawn even if the car wash is thrown in. And if you complete a massive, time-consuming project, an ice cream cone is not commensurate. Be good to yourself. And if my reward is the basketball game, I get to watch the whole game. I do not turn it off at halftime to get going on something else. I promised it to myself, and my word is good.

ADD people have trouble with repetition. Much as we would love to ditch repetitive jobs completely, we cannot. Mowing the lawn, for example, is repetitive. Not only is it a job you have to do over and over, the job itself gets pretty boring the hundredth time you've done it. Rewards are an excellent way to push past the distaste and boredom of performing repetitive tasks.

Deliberately Complement Each Other

Yard work has been an issue of discussion and necessary compromise for Katie and David over the years. The discussion usually moves back and forth between the need to complete the big picture (mowing the lawn) and the ability to pay attention to the important smaller details (weeding and trimming).

David is very good at seeing the big picture. Since the couple live in the country and own several acres of land, mowing the pastures is a recurring task. To David, this job should take precedence over the more detailed lawn work, such as weeding flower beds and trimming bushes. Katie has learned to appreciate his willingness to spend long hours on the riding mower to keep the pastures manicured. But she has also learned that when the flower beds need weeding she had better plan to do them herself, since David fails to notice the weeds. Even when she politely brings them to his attention, he politely tells her he really doesn't care!

Another area they have learned to complement each other is in writing books together. When they begin working on a project, David usually has so many ideas that Katie's head spins. He is a great initiator because his creativity can see many options and his ability to see the big picture helps him to choose the best of those. Next, he and Katie work on an outline together, with David contributing most of the ideas. About that time, though, David begins to lose interest. Now it's Katie's turn to flesh out the ideas and begin fine-tuning the grammar. When they first began writing together, Katie tried to correct all of David's grammatical errors along the way. Each correction brought groans and resentment from David. Thanks to a computer, the stress level in their home is at a manageable level!

Refrain from Fixing Each Other

The first rule then must be, "I will not fix you and you will not fix me." Katie cannot control David's boredom with detail. She'd love to, because it can be very annoying. But not even David can control it. Neither can fix it, tame it, remove it, or banish it to certain times and places.

Let's use the seesaw context again. Both spouses wish their partner would sit closer to the middle. True, both ought to move in toward the middle of the seesaw; there's no denying that. But neither position is superior to the other, and neither can force the other to take up a different position, nor should they.

Accepting your mate's differences requires a degree of tolerance. The second rule then would be, "I will tolerate you, and you tolerate me."

Work to Improve Tolerance

Tolerance is awfully hard as the day grows long, things aren't going well, and everyone is edgy. It's not love. It's not affection. It's not even respect. It's backing off, letting irritations slide by. This is a lot easier for ADD mates to accomplish than for left brainers because the ADD spouse lives so thoroughly in the present. He or she sees, reacts, and then forgets about it. The non-ADD mate, by suppressing irritation, lets it accumulate and build.

You see then the balancing act both mates must perform here. The ADD spouse must not fault the non-ADD mate for pouting or failing to get over an irritation quickly. The non-ADD mate must not conclude that he or she does nothing requiring the mate's tolerance. One might get that idea, the ADD mate puts things behind so easily. Both of you require a large measure of grace and tolerance. Work from that precept.

BUILD APPRECIATION AND RESPECT FOR EACH OTHER

The third rule for balancing well: "I will acknowledge and respect your strengths, and you will do so with mine."

In Katie and David's case, the ability to work together on writing projects rests solidly on this rule. Katie has learned to trust David's creative bursts and insights. She respects his ability to see the big picture, even though there are times when David's propensity toward seeing that big picture seems to steamroll over small but important parts of the puzzle.

David has learned that Katie has a gift for taking abstract ideas and filling in the details that make those concepts become vividly alive and understandable. She would be lost without David's projects and ideas. David, on the other hand, would be lost without her ability to fine tune and organize the entire work. Together, then, a team is born, where both become fulfilled and satisfied. They realize how much they need each other in order to maintain a stable, productive creative process. That's what respect and appreciation are all about.

In every marriage, there must be organization. And whether it is a case in which one person is super-organized and the other disorganized, whether both can order their lives well to an effective degree, they must mesh efforts. We cannot all be as creative as David or as structured as Katie. But that's a matter of degree. We all share the gifts.

"Nice words," an acquaintance said (She's the one who coined *neotomosis* for my office). "Tolerance, respect, all that. But you don't know my spouse. He puts things off. It's not that he can't or forgets. He just doesn't. Procrastination really bugs me! How do I respect something like that?"

CONQUERING PROCRASTINATION

To quote that gray and venerable sage Pogo Possum, "Ain't nothing so urgent today that it won't be urgenter tomorrow."

Ah, Pogo, would that it were so! Pogo spent a goodly amount of time poling through swamps in a flatboat, trolling for bream. What did he know about procrastination?

Procrastination was a significant stumbling block to me throughout my early life. Never put off until tomorrow what you should have done two days ago. However, by mastering an organizational system specifically designed to thwart procrastination, I've finally been able to build credibility with my friends and associates.

Once upon a time, when I would promise to do something, the automatic response was, "Oh, yeah, sure." And even if I did complete what was promised, unless I cared very personally about what needed to be done, the finished product was slipshod at best. Rushed.

Now I'm able to consistently deliver on the demands placed upon me. I have learned, however, to feel the freedom to say, "Call me a couple of days in advance and remind me, please." This request is like a second safety net for me, that nothing might slip through any cracks. I've noticed most people don't mind doing it.

At the core of my system is my appointment book. My paper brain. I make certain that the people with whom I deal know I have a memory problem and that whatever they arrange or say must be written down. Then if I forget to record something, they remind me.

I used to be accused with words similar to these: "A little absentminded, aren't you?" Then I'd wonder what that person was talking about ("Who, me? Huh?") because I had already forgotten about the things I had forgotten!

Here's how my system now works. I am not suggesting that you slavishly copy this system. Far from it. I'm describing what works for me. But your needs are not mine. Using my system as a starting point, build your own. Modify mine, dump it completely, or use it verbatim, but make certain your system is tailored exactly to your needs.

A number of commercial appointment organizing systems are available, such as Daytimer. Preview several before picking what seems to suit you best. Or build one from scratch from a blank notebook.

1. In my daily appointment book I record:
   what I said I would do
   when I said I would do it
   where I said I would deliver it
2. I often record the gist of conversations and phone calls *at the time they are made* so that I don't forget what was said. If this information is written somewhere other than in my appointment book, I note where so I can find it when I need it.
3. Each day is laid out across two facing pages, morning on the left, afternoon and evening on the right. Each page is divided by a vertical line so that the hours appear down the left third of the page. The appointments go there.
4. In the right two thirds of the page, I write the tasks I promised and things I must do. All of them. I also assign each item a priority number in a small circle to the left, rather like a copyright sign. The most important, of course, is number 1, the next number 2, and so on.
5. Here comes the important part. With a highlighter I run a line through each task and appointment completed. That which I have not completed by day's end—the unhighlighted tasks—carry over to the next day.
6. When all the tasks of a day are highlighted, indicating com-

pletion (even if they are completed several days later), I mark an X in the lower right corner of the page. That X has become a coveted reward. I accomplished everything on the page. It's an amazing psychological boost. The more such rewards I earn, the better I feel about whatever I am doing.

7. By Friday, I'm pretty sick of the carryovers and may get them done just to get rid of them. If I have not completed them, I may have to rewrite them for the next week. I hate doing that.

   I don't rewrite them each day. Instead, I carry only their priority numbers forward. That way, I make myself rack my memory and figure out what they were way back there at the beginning of the week or whenever; in that way I make it as uncomfortable as possible to procrastinate, you see. Eventually, my mind game wins, and I get them done and out of the way just to give myself some relief.

   Sometimes as I review the accumulated tasks on Friday, I'll see a job in a different light that either helps me perceive it in greater clarity, making it more do-able, or presents a better way to accomplish it.

8. I must be honest! No fair dumping the job off onto someone else (unless, of course, it's a legitimate delegation) or quietly dropping it from the list. A man's gotta do what a man's gotta do.

The system isn't foolproof. Things slip through cracks. Once in a great while, something slides so long that it's no longer relevant, or worse, it has precipitated a crisis. I still forget now and then to pick up bread and milk. But the method has brought me a long way.

WHERE THE RUBBER HITS THE ROAD

Of all the areas in which organization can make or break a person, money matters reign supreme. If you don't have your financial act together, you're going to be miserable. This has nothing to do with how much you make. It has to do with tax records, and making do, and identifying money leaks.

The ADD adult's personality sort of rubs against the grain of sound money management in a dozen ways. We don't like to plan ahead or think about tomorrow, we don't think before spending impulsively, and we rarely keep adequate records.

It's a disaster waiting to happen! But with the non-ADD mate's support, you can conquer money monsters and succeed in that arena also.

ADDing Money: Financial Management

Jeri speaks:

Rick and I married young. When you're trying to get through school and life is happening quicker than you can keep up with it, money is tight. We had money for school expenses and money for food. That was about it. It was hard to find money for new clothes (which I really cared about). However, Rick usually could come up with a scheme (and a "good" reason) to buy an old motorcycle and fix it up. One time he even talked me into agreeing to sell the diamonds out of my wedding ring to buy us a ski boat. He was extremely persuasive in his arguments, and I guess I really did kind of want that ski boat. But more than that, I was always trying to avoid rocking the boat. But we weren't saving a dime, and not infrequently, at times it looked as if we couldn't keep our heads above water.

Rick speaks:

When we were first married, I loved adventure, variety, and spontaneity—as long as I felt in control of the situation, of course. Jeri wanted to develop a rut as far as I was concerned. She wanted a house, a reliable car, and worst of all she wanted to start a family. To my way of thinking, she wanted to take all the fun out of life. I liked the freedom of living life as it came and staying disentangled from financial and family responsibilities. I resented her desire for stability. There was some envy, too, I think; I envied her ability to make do, no matter how little she had to work with. We got into a lot of loud, highly emotional fights over money.

IMPULSIVITY THE TRAITOR

Some friends of ours—we'll call them Charles and Raye—were going broke without actually buying anything. Charles made a good living, and Raye, a teacher, wasn't doing badly. And yet, they hovered on the verge of bankruptcy. The problem? Their twenty-two-year-old son. Send him to the store for a quart of milk and he was as likely as not to come home with a power boat. This guy had the business acumen of a toddler. The son—call him Joe—was constantly getting in over his head financially.

Charles would bail his son out with an exasperated, "This is the last time, you hear? From now on it's sink or swim"—until the next time.

Joe's tastes weren't extravagant. He didn't buy a Porsche when a Miata would do. He didn't pursue costly hobbies, like yachting or showing five-gaited horses. He was just too impulsive. He could walk into a hardware store for a 3/8-inch bolt and come out with a wheelbarrow (the very thing for relandscaping Dad's yard), a new miter saw (the old one tended to drift off the mark), and a great padded toilet seat that would go perfectly with Mom's new shower curtain. He probably would forget the bolt.

Impulsivity. What a way to shipwreck your financial boat.

Mastering Money

ADD folk will be quick to admit that impulsivity can do them in. Yet most of the time, they are not guilty of extravagance. They have reasons, and often very good reasons, for the purchases they make and expenses they engender. Consider Joe walking into the hardware store. The wheelbarrow really was useful. He lived with his parents still, and he and his dad had been planning for some time to build a terraced flower bed along the north wall of the backyard. You need a wheelbarrow for that. And the miter saw they owned really did tend to drift. The new toilet seat did indeed go perfectly with Mom's bathroom decor. So what was the problem?

Well, had Joe shopped around, he could have picked up a wheelbarrow for $35 instead of the $60 he paid. The miter saw had been one of those one-project tools, and they really didn't have further use for one in the foreseeable future. Had Joe given it some thought, he would have appreciated that the existing toilet seat also fit the bathroom decor well. In fact, Mom liked her old one better. When he brought home the new one, she was faced with a dilemma: keep her old one and hurt her son's feelings, or install one she liked less. Joe never intended to cause her a problem that way; he just didn't think.

And they still needed a 3/8-inch bolt.

ADD people have to treat money with the care that everyone else gives it, only more so. That is, they follow the same rules as non-ADD folk, but they have to make the rules more stringent and follow them more closely. The attitude should be to curb impulsivity and replace some (but not all) of the natural enthusiasm with the restraint of wisdom. Here are five steps that can help.

God Comes First

When Jeri and I were growing up, both of our families put God's needs ahead of their own. So a part of our money picture from the very beginning of our marriage included giving a percentage off the top to God's work. Neither of us had an argument there.

You know, God honors that. He always honors that. There are many people who don't believe in the tithe or some other system for returning to God what is His, and that's all right. Let each person and couple act as they feel is right. But when I talk about money matters as they pertain to Jeri and me, devoting a percentage of our income comes first. It's the way we operate.

Don't Allow Indebtedness

If you don't have the money, don't buy it. It's such a simple, simple precept, and it's so hard for an ADD person to follow. This one rule in itself would have kept Joe out of financial hot water. Had he taken just enough money to the hardware store to pay for a bolt, he would have come out with a bolt. Unfortunately, he took his credit card.

There are important exceptions to this rule. When you're buying a house, it may be financially wise to pay into a mortgage, depending on interest rates and other such financial factors. The monetary advantages then outweigh the disadvantage of indebtedness. It may be wiser in your particular circumstance to lease a vehicle rather than buy it. You can sit down with a sharp pencil and figure things like that out.

The indebtedness Jeri and I avoid is the kind that allows us to buy something when we don't have the money to buy it with. A boat. A new car when the old one works just fine. Beware a credit card that's warm to the touch.

We are not suggesting credit cards are bad. They are the best way to cover expenses when you're traveling, for example, or when it is unwise to carry large amounts of money. We do recommend that you have the money to pay off the credit card balance in full each month. The month you cannot pay the balance in full is the month you put *all* the credit cards away in a drawer until you're ahead again. All of them, not just the unpaid one. No exceptions.

DEVISE A TWENTY-FOUR-HOUR RULE

Maybe at your house it should be a forty-eight-hour rule. Whatever the time frame, here is a dandy curb to impulsivity. When you spot something in a store that screams, "Buy me! Buy me!" you make note of it and go home. If at least a day later the scream is still as loud, maybe you might go buy it. It's a cooling-off period.

What do you do in those intervening twenty-four or forty-eight hours? The time allows you to ask a few questions you wouldn't have time for if you bought on impulse.

Can I do better elsewhere?

The same product or an equivalent may be available for less money at some other outlet. If buying it is really a good idea, if it's an item you really could use or enjoy, then it's worth shopping around for.

Is it really going to complete my happiness the way I'm sure it will?

That's a facetious question, actually. But the intent is valuable. Will this item actually improve anything? Will it make our home more beautiful, our lives richer, our day-to-day work easier, etc.? Asking this question is a good way to avoid ending up with that cute little stuffed armadillo that looked so great in the souvenir shop and doesn't fit in your Danish Modern decor at all.

Remember how badly impulsivity can trip up the ADD person; it's that impulsivity you are fighting. Impulsive people also tend to lose enthusiasm quickly; that is, what looked great today loses its luster tomorrow. Employing the twenty-four-hour rule makes use of the ADD person's own tendency to lose interest in something in a short time. It allows some of the luster to dull.

What do others say?

Others' advice is pretty lusterless, too, when you have your heart set on something. Cheer up. I'm not suggesting you have to follow every piece of advice you get. Far from it. But you should pause long enough to *get* it. I learned after long and hard experience to listen to what Jeri has to say. I may not agree with her; in fact, I usually don't. But I now recognize that her hesitation in a situation is usually very well-founded. Often her casual comments are sufficient to give me pause.

What does the bank account say?

Bank accounts speak volumes. If you can't write a check to cover it without withdrawing a chunk from savings, the twenty-four-hour rule gives you time to come to grips with the fact that you can't afford it just now. That's a hard thing to accept, especially for the ADD buyer. The ADD person doesn't like strictures, and a pinched money supply is among the tightest of strictures. Waiting before purchasing allows time for the reality to sink in. ADD people in particular need that extra time.

When is the wisest time to obtain this item?

There are occasions when the impulse buy that looks so great just now really is a good, sound purchase—some other time. You can buy a swimsuit when the new fashions come out and prices are premium, or you can buy a swimsuit during a season-end sale. You need the swimsuit. The question becomes one of timing. Again, the twenty-four-hour rule gives you enough breathing space that you can consider the timing.

What about the budget?

For the ADD person, budgeting is a sham. It's the very antithesis of all we stand for. We don't like the limitations of a stinkin' budget, and we won't put up with it!

To our frequent woe, budgeting is one of those things, like root canals and traffic snarls, we must deal with. The ADD adult who submits to the tyranny of a budget succeeds.

DEVELOP AN IRONCLAD BUDGET

Jeri is a superb budgeter. Here is where I had to make a powerful change. I had to force myself to submit to her budget directives. My head knew I ought to. My head knew I didn't stand a ghost of a chance of maintaining a budget on my own. But my heart rebelled. For once, I made my heart submit to my head. That doesn't happen often.

A budget is worthless unless it is inviolate. We had friends, fellow students back in the salad days, who faithfully wrote out a budget for the week and the month and the year. But they loved clothes. With a snicker, they'd boast that in September they'd already spent October and November's clothes money. Or even next year's. Obviously, their so-called budget was a paper exercise designed to assuage a guilty conscience. I'm sorry to report that they've since divorced. Their constant financial straits, in part, drove them apart.

Budgeting is nothing more than planning ahead, and it's not the only way to do so. That's the ADD person's downfall—planning. By planning ahead, I mean not just next week's food and rent, but *way* ahead.

People who are self-employed must put aside quarterly estimated income tax. They have to send in that estimated tax payment even when they don't know for certain that it is the right amount. Maybe income will take a dive and they will have overpaid. Maybe God's blessings will bless the IRS. They do the best they can with their limited vision of the future.

That's the kind of planning I mean, not just for the self-employed but for everyone, ADD people in particular. You look into the future through smudged glasses and figure out where your money is going to go. (Speaking of estimated tax, self-employed ADD people have a real problem with sending in quarterly payments when so many other things cry out for the money. I'd like to know sometime what percentage of people who get stuck with a large tax bill come April are ADD people; the proportion has got to be high.)

Planning takes many forms. For example, if you are a two-income family, plan some way to live on one income and put back the other income for the kids' college costs, retirement, buying a house . . . You get the idea.

Having specific goals in mind helps curb casual or careless spending in the present. ADD people may well want to write out long-term goals and objectives—a sort of super-budget—and keep them *with* the credit card or checkbook. We aren't going to remember them spontaneously when some attractive potential impulse buy begins its siren song.

If that's what it takes, give the financial reins over to the mate. This is awfully tough for any husband, but for an ADD male it's particularly onerous. Asking an ADD adult to give up financial control is like asking a jockey to ride an unbridled horse in a race. The jockey will scratch before he'll take a risk like that. The ADD adult will turn purple, for starters. And yet, in the long run, this may be the very point upon which marital happiness pivots.

Susanna Wesley, mother of John Wesley, was lockstep left-brain. She married a man, Samuel, who showed all the signs of Attention Deficit Disorder. He didn't wait until he made money before he'd spend it. She spent her whole married life in penury and debt. After Samuel died, her children sold the furnishings to satisfy the debt, and she lived modestly and well from then on, never to owe another penny. Had Samuel been able to surrender finances to his wife, she could have raised their children—she bore nineteen babies; ten reached maturity—debt-free. But that was three hundred years ago, and Susanna faced handicaps of culture as well as her husband's impulsivity.

Today, the housewife has her counterpart in the househusband, and a good many financial advisors are female. In our culture it does not matter who handles the money, non-ADD wife or non-ADD husband. Sit down together, therefore, and write a pact. To take the sting out of it, put a time limit on it. At the end of that time, sit down together again and either extend the agreement or rewrite it.

> *I, _____, surrender control of*
> *the checkbook, savings account(s), money market*
> *accounts, and other financial instruments in our family. I*
> *will put my full paycheck into account _____*
> *except for a stipend of $_____ from each*
> *check. The maximum I will put on credit cards each*
> *week is $_____ and I will keep all credit slips.*
> *We both agree to make no purchases over*
> *$_____ without the consent of the other party.*

(Signatures)

There is hope, however, for the ADD adult who sees nothing but monetary hunger and budget constraints down the road. Try building a kitty.

FEED A MAD-MONEY KITTY

Control is a big issue with ADD folk, and spur-of-the-moment is most appealing. So we maintain a mad-money kitty. It is to be spent on fun things, frivolous things, the things that ADD people love most. That is, you salt away a little in a separate fund so that the ADD mate can indulge recklessly once in a while. You cannot imagine the sense of release that periodic fling provides. The ADD mate no longer feels as if he or she is in a monetary straitjacket all the time. Certainly you can't fritter away the whole income impulsively, but here's a little chunk of money that you can indeed use whimsically. In the ADD adult's case, where whim looms so prominently, it is not a waste, no matter how it is spent. It's a satisfying tool.

Find Contentment by Winning the Game

ADD folk by nature are restless, ever ready to reach out, almost never content with the status quo. Contentment usually does not come easily for us. And yet, contentment is perhaps the single greatest curb on reckless spending.

"Why should I go shopping when I don't need anything?" No merchant can counter that simple logic, although heaven knows they try.

And therein lies a secret. The ADD person just loves games, and merchandising is a big game. One of the biggest. The merchant is trying to lure you in to buy something you don't need even while you're resisting the impulse to buy. Who's going to win?

When the ADD adult approaches purchasing in that way, resistance gets a lot easier. We're poor losers. And when the merchant wins by luring us into an unwise purchase, we lose. Once we grasp that game plan, we strive to win. From there on, the merchants might win a battle now and then, but we'll be victors in the war.

Maintaining contentment can be tough, however. We ADD types have a real struggle with contentment. It doesn't come easily. Reason doesn't make much of an impression. "I should be content because I have what I need" is excellent philosophy, it's even excellent theology, but it doesn't sink into the ADD adult well.

About the only way to engender contentment is to develop a spirit of thanksgiving. It's not an instant fix. But a spirit of gratitude, over the long haul, will breed contentment. I needn't mention that you have to be sincere. When you thank God for something, you'd better be sincere. But that doesn't mean it can't be fun as well.

"Thank you, God, for our lawnmower. Now you may have noticed, God, that the shaft is bent ever since I accidentally went over that low stump. It cuts on a slant and it's just plain dangerous. Still, it's served many good years and for that we earnestly do thank you. If you would direct us to a hardware store sale on lawnmowers, we'd appreciate it."

There was nothing tongue-in-cheek about that particular petition—sincere all the way. The lawnmower did indeed serve us faithfully right up to the end. And we were indeed grateful. And I didn't even see that low little stump in the grass before the *whunk!* and the sudden ringing silence.

There are hundreds—no, thousands—of things around you that you've never expressed appreciation for. Expressing that appreciation will promote contentment as nothing else can. It focuses your attention squarely upon what you have, not what you think you want.

Can you achieve that kind of a goal? It's possible. Certainly so. Think of Albert Einstein, my fellow ADD achiever. He wore a comfortable old sweater. He normally walked to work. Incidentally, the mother-in-law of a friend, now eighty, says she worked as a cleaning woman in the same building where Einstein held lectures. On occasion they would meet in the elevator. Dr. Einstein would politely greet her and she him. Says she, "That man lived the equality he preached." He was content.

So was Sam Walton, the man behind Wal-Mart and Sam's Club and one of the wealthiest men in the world. He could have bought out Donald Trump, but he lived modestly because he was content. It can be done. You the ADD adult can do it.

Still and all, a whole lot of anger can be generated over the subject of money. Anger, like money, is more manageable if you come at it as a game. But that doesn't always work. There are, however, tricks that do.

SEVEN

ADDmitting Anger

Jeri speaks:
   Anger used to be such a big problem with us. And this is the one area where Rick has changed the most. Early in our marriage he was often verbally abusive. Now I can attribute that more to his impulsivity than to a mean spirit, but that didn't make it any nicer then. Once he realized how much this harmed our relationship, he really faced the problem head-on. When he lost his temper and said unkind things (actually, *shouted* unkind things would be more accurate), he willingly apologized.

   I know this isn't supposed to be a preachy book, but there is no other way for me to explain it: God changed Rick's heart. Rick began to put himself in my shoes, to care about my feelings, and to understand what Scripture says about honoring your wife.

   I notice that he often diffuses tense situations now with humor. Where he used to use sarcasm against me, he is able to find genuine, sweet humor in a situation, and it has often saved the day—and the night!

Rick speaks:

A lot of comedians use the differences between men and women as grist for their routines, and there's a good reason—we're so different. When Jeri and I married, our differences became apparent very quickly—by this I mean emotional differences and differences of style. Good old me, I just assumed she was that way because she was a woman, and you know—women are more emotional, they have moods . . .

It took me a long time to see the truth. When the light finally dawned that I was using anger as a club and with that club was hurting my family and others terribly—it wasn't any preconceived difference between men and women after all—I learned much about myself. My initial reaction to an angering situation or injustice is a biggie—either blow up or withdraw from the situation completely. I withdraw more now, rather than let my anger get out of hand. But it wasn't always so. Anger management is a long, hard trail to hike.

THE ANGER PROBLEM

Arnie and Eva looked forward to the Christmas holidays. Their friends Abe and Sarah were going to spend the holiday week with them in their new home outside Dallas. They hadn't seen Abe and Sarah for three years, ever since they moved out here from Ohio. Money was tight, but the visit was worth a few sacrifices.

The day after Christmas, Arnie and Eva brought their old friends home from Dallas-Fort Worth International. They were rejoicing! They yakked. They swam in the heated pool. They feasted. Yakked. Played Uno. Yakked some more. Three days passed happily.

Eva's food budget had been spent, but the food was running out. All of it. She had grossly underestimated what four cheerful people would eat. Just the noshing was impressive. While the other three went sight-seeing, she headed for the grocery to restock on essentials like diet cola, popcorn, meat, and potatoes.

She arrived home at about the same time the others did. Abe and Sarah each picked up grocery bags and headed for the house. Eva would have, but Arnie exploded in her face.

"For crying out loud, how much did you spend? There has to be ten bags of stuff here! You keep telling me we don't have that kind of money, and look at this! *How could you be so stupid?!*" Fulminating like the basso villain in an opera, Arnie roared off into the house.

Eva knew Abe and Sarah heard every word of the outburst clearly. Residents of San Antonio heard clearly. In one wicked swoop, Arnie had humiliated both her and their guests and cast a cold, dark shadow across the week of happiness. Eva sat down on the back bumper and wept, as much from fury as from humiliation.

I don't have to tell you that Arnie was an ADD adult. The situation actually occurred, but I changed names and a few other facts. Believe me. It happens. For an ADD mate, instant, intense anger always lies in the shadow, just waiting to leap out and ruin something.

ADD mates are, by and large, reactors. A balloon is a reactor. There it lies, limp, until you inflate it. Blow it up and bring it into contact with a sharp needle—*bang*. That's what I mean by reactor. The balloon does not think about the pin, or how to respond if the point gets too close—*bang*. The balloon cannot help itself; it cannot do anything besides—*bang*—react.

That's the way ADD adults are. The kids, too.

Complicating the picture is the fact that ADD people and non-ADD mates handle long-term anger differently. The ADD person blows sky high quickly and promptly forgets all about it. Here's the non-ADD mate seething for the next three days, and the ADD spouse doesn't even remember the blow-up.

What's going on? Quite a bit, and at the same time, not

enough. We believe one of the reasons ADD people are inattentive is because their neurotransmitters, the chemicals that make the momentary connection between brain nerve cells, are in short supply. Without bountiful neurotransmitter chemicals, some connections don't get made. We talk about studying hard or thinking hard. That's exactly true. A lot of neurons—that is, brain cells—are torching off appropriately when the average person concentrates on a problem or a learning situation.

This same situation exists where anger is involved. Initiating action, which is the opposite of reacting, takes a lot of fast thinking. *Why must I act quickly? What will be the result?* That all goes on almost instantly. The thinker then moderates, stifles, or allows the release of a response—anger or whatever. This is not to say that every left brainer beautifully controls every reaction. It is to say that non-ADD people have some modest mechanism for doing so. ADD adults do not.

The neurotransmitter-impoverished ADD adult does not have the luxury of a natural rapid-fire assessment of appropriate response. When the world accuses ADD reactors of failing to think first, that's exactly the problem.

Other factors enter in also. Because of that short attention span, the ADD adult will either forget or miss altogether the dozen positive things that happened and react only to this most recent single negative thing. Obviously, nothing is going his or her way, everything is rotten, and anger is a response to this mistaken frustration.

In short, ADD adults have trouble reaching the same level of maturity as most other people. We get stuck emotionally at kid level and don't always deal with problems in mature ways. The ADD mate's attitudes seem hopelessly intransigent to the non-ADD spouse. Fortunately, resolution is possible.

RESOLVING THE PROBLEM

Here is where an ADD adult and non-ADD mate must enter into a tenuous partnership. I say tenuous because responding to anger with anger is so very, very human, and the non-ADD mate is very human. You might say the two of them will ask each other to become superhuman. That is tenuous because it doesn't always work. And yet, a moderate or even modest success rate is so much better than no success at all, it is worth every effort to work beyond the natural interactions of the ADD adult and mate—anger begetting anger.

Of the five or so elements with which the ADD adult and mate can overcome anger and outbursts, understanding is the basis.

Understanding

It helps, it really does, to realize what's going on. That's one form of understanding. The ADD adult grasps that he has no physiological mechanism for moderating anger available such as the non-ADD person has. Whom that realization *really* helps is the non-ADD mate; it helps that spouse muster a bit more patience and tolerance, for the person knows the ADD mate is working from a disadvantage. Together the ADD adult and mate understand that the ADD adult has to come from way behind if she or he is going to clamp a lid on those outbursts.

Another factor to understand is that business about control. Every human being needs to feel in control of something, his or her own life for starters. Even little children who are not wise enough to use control safely yearn to seize it. Adults, it seems, always hunger for more control in their lives, no matter how much they have. ADD adults have precious little control; they claw at all they can get.

ADD adults and their mates already understand about control needs. What the ADD mate in particular must grasp is that explosive anger is a jim-dandy control technique, and she is probably using it in just that way. You blow up instantly and blow up frighteningly, and people back off. They acquiesce. They defer. The ADD adult who erupts in fury is likely to get his wishes; that's heady power. Do non-ADD adults use anger that way? Sure they do. But it's usually not hair-trigger; it's more often a considered technique. The ADD adult is grasping for that handful of control at gut-level, with no input from the reasoning mind.

To see what is happening in an exploding situation even as the explosion is occurring—that calls for superhuman effort. Either the non-ADD mate or the ADD partner might realize what is happening—you might call it a light-bulb-turning-on revelation. As soon as the light comes on, the person with the realization yells "Stop!" It may well be the exploding partner. Anything to abort the fury.

To stop such chaos in midcourse takes superhuman power, and that's why I say that the ADD adult and mate are asking an enormous amount of each other.

But here's the kicker: the ADD adult is into control, and we are now talking about the ultimate in power-wielding. To slow and control an act of anger is the most impressive, severe, and godly control of all. If you can pull off something like that, you have the iron grip of a world tyrant.

To the ADD adult who loves games and challenges and the new and different, controlling anger becomes possible when it becomes a challenge. Understanding what is happening while it happens is what enables the ADD adult to apply the brakes. Control makes the brakes work. It's not surefire, especially in the beginning. But it's a thrilling feeling of victory when you can pull it off.

Not all anger is explosive, of course. There is also the slow burn born of frustration or circumstance that so easily becomes a fast burn. You have a better shot at controlling this kind of anger because you have a little time to work on it. Time really helps because to handle that kind of anger requires self-talk and an adjustment in some very basic attitudes. It takes time to talk to yourself and make the adjustments.

Adjusting Your Belief System

How's this for an object lesson? I was scheduled to speak on a radio talk show. I left for the studio about forty-five minutes early, because the host was a friend of mine and I wanted a little time at the front end to relax with him, chat, enjoy his company. I'm cruising down the freeway and life is good.

And then traffic comes to a complete halt. I'm trapped in a highway-turned-parking lot about halfway between exits. Word filters back that an oil truck has overturned in the road. Also, there's something about chickens. Pretty soon some chickens start filtering back too. Frantic white blobs. I can just picture one of those big chicken trucks being involved in the pileup ahead. Do you know how many chickens fit in a flatbed trailer full of chicken crates? Thousands! I'm picturing a bezillion chickens fouled in the oil spill from the tank truck, and all these stranded motorists coerced into a chicken cleanup, the way volunteers clean up loons and ducks in a coastal oil tanker spill.

My amusement fades pretty quickly. It's been fifteen minutes, and here we sit. My palms sweat. Out loud, I'm telling those bozos to get a move on. I doubt they hear me; they're a mile or so up ahead.

Half an hour. My teeth are clenched, and I'm pounding on the dashboard. Let me tell you, when anger slips in and takes over, you are totally taken over. Totally. And you don't even realize what's happening. I was *howling* mad! Just howling.

Let's pause in this miserable mini-drama for a moment to analyze what's going on here. A revolver provides a good example.

When you fire a revolver, you pull the trigger and the bullet comes out, right? Sort of. Actually, a lot happens between the time you squeeze the trigger and the bullet leaves the barrel. The cylinder rotates a sixth of a turn, bringing a shell under the hammer. Meanwhile, the hammer rears back and slams forward. It strikes the bullet's brass casing, and all sorts of chemical reactions take place, the end being that an explosion inside the casing blows the lead slug out the barrel.

Anger works just about the same way. There's the trigger event, the thing that precipitates the anger in the first place. The reaction, the flying bullet, is the display of anger. But in between the precipitating event and the display, an awful lot goes on that you don't consciously notice. That is what, for lack of a better term, I'll call the belief system.

The belief system is all the thought that goes on in between a precipitating event and a person's reaction to that event. It's a filter, if you will, or a thought-shaping device. It's the things we believe deep down inside that make us think the way we do.

So let's look again at my story. The trigger event was that oil truck accident and the resulting traffic snarl. The reaction was my rapidly escalating anger as the delay dragged on.

But just as a trigger cannot fire a bullet directly, so a trigger event cannot induce anger directly. It's that belief system in between that controls the anger, just as all the events which follow the squeeze of the trigger determine whether the bullet will ever leave the chamber. A lot of things in a revolver can cause a misfire; if the hammer doesn't work right, if a spring is weak, if for some reason the shell is faulty, it won't go off.

You control escalating anger, therefore, by controlling the belief system, by interfering with the revolver somewhere between the trigger and the casing.

So what did I believe that could make me so furious I was pounding on the dashboard?

- That my friend the talk show host would think less of me if I failed to show on time.
- That the radio program would be reduced to a shambles if I wasn't there to be the guest.
- That I would be humiliated by showing late or not at all.
- Most of all, that I was not in control. There wasn't a thing I could do about the situation. I was helpless.

I had plenty of time to sort this stuff out as I sat there beneath the blazing sun, but the analysis didn't take all that long, really. It was not the spilled oil truck making me angry; it was this combination of beliefs.

Were they facts? Realities?

Hey, my friend knows that if I'm stuck between exits in the middle of a traffic mess, it's nothing personal. Of course he would not think less of me. And if he did, it would be his problem, not mine. I was blameless. In fact, I'd left early.

And who am I that the radio program is going to collapse if I'm not there? As entertaining and informative and likeable as old Rick Fowler might be, the world of radio can get along just fine without him.

It's not humiliating to get unavoidably stuck in traffic.

Control is an issue I've been fighting my whole life, an old and familiar foe. I was fighting it now. No big deal there.

None of those realizations was particularly comforting to my ego, but they were valid, all the same. As the middlemen, they were generating the anger just as the falling hammer and not the trigger actually detonates the bullet. Alter them, get rid of them, and the anger is defused. File down the hammer a little, and the revolver looks just fine—except that it won't fire.

And that's exactly what I did. I went down through the belief system, as I just reviewed, analyzing and identifying my attitudes. Let me recommend that you do so prayerfully. Addressing the problem from an attitude of prayer puts God's hand in yours and smooths the way greatly. When I finished looking at my predicament prayerfully, I asked God's forgiveness for my anger.

The cars up ahead began to move. In slow motion we inched past the overturned oil truck. We saw no bedraggled chickens reminiscent of the Exxon Valdez spill. Apparently the chickens had come from a little pickup truck with one broken poultry crate.

I arrived at the studio only four minutes late and with a glorious story to tell. I had made peace; I was in tune with God and was able, therefore, to do my best.

But you can handle anger a step before it reaches the trigger stage, and that's by identifying the triggers themselves. Realize which trigger is involved, and you can cut the anger off at the pass, as they used to say in the shoot-'em-up westerns. Different things torque different people. They can't all be important. How do you sort it out?

Prioritizing Anger Triggers

So what burns you up? Most of the stuff the kids do, usually. Kids can drive me out of my tree when the day is otherwise going roughly anyway. So I've divided all the reasons the kids might make me angry into three categories:

- absolutes
- house rules
- personal preference or convenience

Absolutes are things the kid doesn't get away with ever. That can range from running out into the street to theft. They involve either ethics, sin, or personal peril. Anger is actually a manifestation of fear, and here is where the fear is greatest; my child will err grievously before God and man or be killed through carelessness or foolhardiness.

House rules have to be set up and written out clearly, so that parents and kids alike know what's what. You don't bring a friend home and trash the garage. You don't dig up the yard. We want the children to learn respect for others and for property, and house rules teach a lot of that.

Personal preference or convenience—that's where most of my kids' infractions fall. Leaving the hall light on isn't a major sin; it annoys me, that's all. Making noise when I want to watch the news is annoying. I can ask them to go elsewhere or use the TV in the back of the house, but I've no right to become angry.

As an example of personal convenience, consider this little play:

ME: (Angrily) Do you *have* to get cookie crumbs all over the rug like that?

CHIP: (Innocently) So what? The dog will get 'em.
        (Enter dog on cue. Dog eagerly licks up the crumbs and
        sits down as close to Chip's knee as he can, waiting for
        further largess.)

So where's the reason for anger? You see, for an ADD adult, minor annoyances can trigger just as much anger as major infractions, and that's what I have to battle. I fight the fight with a lot of self-talking, mostly along the lines of, "I have no reason or right to get angry over this."

What twists your knobs? Think about your various anger triggers. Then think about how important they really are. Prioritizing them won't cure all the outbursts, but it sure helps.

Knowing yourself a little better helps resolve the anger problem also. ADD adults are famous for romping merrily through life without noticing things other people feel and see instantly— things like hunger, weariness, and stress. Yet those physical conditions, if you will, can escalate anger appreciably.

Reading Your Body

A friend noticed this subhead, "reading your body." She smirked. "But I don't have any tattoos."

No, but she has body cues, and so do you. ADD adults are particularly vulnerable to fatigue, stress, and hunger. When we miss meals or get overtired, we get cranky. Everyone does that. But we are often not attuned to recognizing that we are running on fumes. Our body is saying, "Feed me," or "Rest me," and we blindly charge ahead. Our hyperactivity keeps us going physically even when we're fatigued. Whereas most people feel stress or weariness coming on and do something about it, we fail to even notice. We don't like routine and are usually not sticky about when meals are served. It all adds up.

To avoid severe anger, then, the ADD adult or the non-ADD mate (which is more often the case) is wise to consider points such as the following:

- How many hours since the last good calorie intake? Is there a reason blood sugar levels ought to be down? Low blood sugar encourages grumpiness and, therefore, anger.
- Did you rest well last night? Did you feel vaguely cheated this morning because you didn't get the kind of rest you'd expect from a night's sleep?
- Did you get enough bed time? For example, a volunteer fire fighter called out on a fire at two A.M. isn't going to be Pollyanna when he or she gets in at five, facing a day in the trenches. He got adequate rest while in bed but wasn't in bed long enough.
- What's going on in your life that would upset someone with more delicate sensibilities than yours?

Note, I didn't say "What's upsetting you?" The ADD adult might quite honestly respond, "Nothing," because that person doesn't notice anything. "Oh, that. That's nothing," she'll say. The truth is, it might be upsetting her below the surface. The ADD adult was simply too preoccupied to see it. Keep that preoccupation in mind, always. Look on it, again, as a control issue. You don't want situations and stress-producers controlling you, especially when you don't even realize it.

If you want to control anger, pay closer attention to body needs and messages, therefore. The ADD adult is at enough disadvantage without letting impaired thought and responses add their toll. As much as you might dislike routine, keeping regular meals and bedtime hours can help anger management immensely.

No technique or self-talk can quell anger 100 percent of the time, and it shouldn't. Anger is real, it happens, it serves a purpose, and it must be vented. What we seek to control is inappropriate anger and overreaction.

Arnie's reaction to Eva's grocery purchase was not only over-kill, it was inappropriate. She was doing what had to be done.

He was criticizing where no criticism was deserved. That's the kind of anger that needs to be controlled.

But it was not. So now what do you do?

Mending Fences

For the sake of what he held dear—his marriage and his friendships—Arnie had to do some fence mending, and the quicker the better. But if Arnie is typical, he didn't even notice the fences were broken.

The ADD spouse may well feel a matter is ended as soon as his initial fury has abated. That person must come to realize it just isn't so. The non-ADD mate is almost certainly still fuming. Not only is the original source of anger still rankling, the non-ADD mate resents the ADD spouse's ability to get over the situation so quickly and casually.

The healing balm here is understanding and communication. You've heard that a million times, but in this particular situation it's the one and only thing that will work.

"I'm furious with you, [ADD mate], and have been for three days." The non-ADD mate must speak up. Air the resentment.

The ADD spouse's responsibility is to accept that, whether he or she can appreciate how anger can fester in someone else. "I don't understand, but I believe you."

Talk it out.

Above all, exercise forgiveness freely in both directions. Ask it and offer it. Forgiveness is the best anger-snuffer going. For the incident I described with Arnie and Eva there in the beginning, forgiveness would be the only good emollient for restoring the situation. Arnie must ask forgiveness from Eva, and also from Abe and Sarah.

By forgiveness, of course, I am talking about sincere forgiveness. A few words tossed out glibly ain't gonna cut it. Remorse and repentance must accompany a true spirit of forgiving and asking forgiveness. It need not be overdone or too elaborate for the occasion. Appropriate dosages will do the trick just fine.

I have learned as I get better about dealing with life that the more secure I feel about myself, the less I feel the need to get angry. That's greatly liberating. In fact, I can even measure the health of my sense of self, if you will, by watching how easily I anger. The truly secure adult doesn't have to fuss and fume.

That doesn't cure the hair-trigger responses, the constant motion others may find annoying, and the impulsivity, however. Nothing cures impulsivity and hyperactivity. There are ways, though, to harness them and sometimes to even control them.

EIGHT

ADDjusting to Hyperactivity and Impulsivity

Jeri speaks:

Talking to Rick can be like trying to score in skeet shooting when there're five clay birds in the air at once. You spend most of your time with your head swinging back and forth, figuring out where the target is. He is getting much better now because he's really trying to be better about it. But when I first knew him, he was never still a second.

We'd sit down for a serious discussion about some major topic. First his hands would get busy. He'd rearrange whatever was on the table, or maybe tie his shoes. Not that they were untied to start with. Suddenly he's on his feet and chugging across the room. He gets something off a shelf. He ricochets off the wall, sits in a chair twenty feet away a few moments, leaps up and ricochets off another wall. By this time my nerves are threatening to make my voice scream. And then, believe it or not, he's leaving the room! Then in he pops again. This is a serious discussion? It is to laugh. Or cry.

He doesn't leave the room anymore, thank heaven. And I have learned that he is not ignoring me when he's dancing on the ceiling like that. In fact, he's paying much better attention when he's moving around than when he's sitting still. I've finally adjusted to the fact that for Rick, to talk is to think, and to think is to move.

Rick speaks:
    Jeri blew up once when I was a little too active and intense and yelled, "Why don't you relax?" Okay. So I mowed the lawn and greased the car. Then she *really* got upset.
    Jeri is not a particularly phlegmatic person—that is, overly cautious, sedentary, and slow. In fact she's quite active, riding horses, getting out and doing things, keeping a heavy schedule and accomplishing many tasks well. But she can sit still when sitting is appropriate, and she gets tired. It used to bother her a lot that I never sat and I seemed never to slow down and unwind. Actually, I do get tired, but my body just keeps moving until I slam it into the bed and make it quit.
    And impulsiveness! Jeri is measured and wise in decisions. Not sluggish or indecisive, but thoughtful. I get an idea and I'm off and running with it. For example, I got this idea to liquidate. In a matter of weeks I'd sold the boat, one of our cars, and the house. We were liquid all right, and in thirty days we were going to be standing out in the street. Every now and then, Jeri takes a dim view of my ideas. That was one of those times.

THE ACTIVE MATE

Not all ADD adults are hyperactive. Most are. Not all hyperactive children have ADD. Many do. All ADD adults, however, are impulsive to some degree, usually a great degree. When you combine impulsivity with hyperactivity, you have popcorn in a popper without a lid—never knowing which kernel is going to pop next or where it will fly.
    For purposes of this chapter, let's assume we're talking about

the ADD adult who is hyperactive, rather than having to say, "Although not all ADD adults are, the person who is hyperactive blah, blah, blah" all the time.

There are serious disadvantages to living with a person in perpetual motion; there are disadvantages to *being* that person. But there are delightful advantages as well. I'd like to look at the advantages and the disadvantages, and then look at solutions with which to ameliorate the problems.

Advantages

When your car's timing is off and you need it adjusted (better change the timing chain, too; it's been 50,000 miles), do you want the mechanic to be a lethargic, drawling fellow who stares at your engine while he contemplates the vacation to Hawaii this is going to pay for? Or do you want an energetic guy who will dive under the hood, change the chain, and have it on their electronic heart-lung machine before you can get a cup of coffee in the waiting room?

Where promptness pays and the job offers variety, as in an auto repair shop, nobody is better than a hyperactive. Impulsiveness doesn't hinder the work a bit. And when the repair job requires some thought, or an unusual answer (let's say you have a classic Impala and the part you need is no longer available), the ADD adult is your person. We're great at coming up with the creative solutions.

What we crave is a rich variety of small tasks. We want to see the fruit of our labors immediately. We don't want repetition. The mechanic like the one I just described who does so well in a repair shop working on a wide variety of vehicle problems would not be good in a mini-lube shop doing the same job over and over on a zillion cars a day. Sure, they're small tasks, but they're all essentially the same one. Likely as not, that energetic fellow is probably not very diligent in restoring a classic car; as skills go, he's certainly up to the challenge of the work, but the task takes too long. In fact, he probably has two or three old clunkers lying about, and they're going to be wonderful—once they're restored.

Someday.

Hyperactives and impulsives do very well in emergency services positions such as emergency room doctor or nurse, paramedic or emergency medical technician, fire fighter, police officer—street cop, not desk jockey—or soldiers. These people handle the initial problem—it requires quick reflexes, quick action, and snap decisions—and then pass it on to someone else for the long-range attention. Perfect.

ADD individuals also do well under the kind of sudden, strident stress that makes blithering ninnies out of some people. We can be on a problem in a moment and act instinctively. Call it impulsively. But if we're trained, making the impulse act appropriate, we're the ones you want when chaos threatens.

Incidentally, street cops we might be, but not private investigators. Contrary to folk wisdom and popular literature, private investigators spend almost all their time sifting through arcane records or sitting on surveillance. That's not the ADD adult's way.

If the ADD adult is dissatisfied with present work, she might keep an eye out for positions that fit her predispositions better. There is no sense for a person to chafe in an irritating job, trying to fit her roundness into some square hole, when there are so many jobs that the person can do extremely well. Such positions will feature nonrepetitive work, a variety of challenges, fast turnaround time on individual projects or mini-tasks, and a minimum of delicate tact when dealing with others.

There certainly are such jobs. How about a fellow who makes corrective footwear? He works in a small shoe factory in Pennsylvania. He can work any machine in the shop. He starts with a piece of leather and the mold of a person's feet and builds a pair of shoes, one corrective and the other "normal." "No two are alike," he claims. "I've served babies and old men, disabled people and athletes."

See what I mean?

Also, we're usually pretty quick workers when the work interests us. The neighbor of a friend of mine mows his lawn at a trot. No fooling. I've watched him. He's constantly scurrying around out there; his yard means everything to him, and it's always trimmed and cleared to perfection. In autumn, the squirrels in the conifers cut green cones and drop them. He's out there picking the cones up before the squirrels can get down out of the trees to retrieve them.

In short, we hyperactive folks are extremely good at jobs that fit our activity patterns, both paid work and at-home tasks. We're proud of our work, too.

But now I have to admit, sometimes—just rarely, just barely— there's a wee, tiny little down side to hyperactivity and impulsivity. *Really* tiny.

Disadvantages

A friend relates this observation: "There's this big black Newfoundland dog down the street. I mean big! Some dogs sneak up onto the sofa. She *is* the sofa. She behaves really dignified because she moves so casually. Almost never runs. Just strolls along while everything hurries out of her way. Across the street is one of those miniature cockapoos. Yap, yap, yap, constantly running around on those four-inch legs. Our three-year-old was terrified of the cockapoo, but she wasn't the least bit afraid of the Newfoundland. She's eight now. She's still reserved about the little dog and loves the big one."

That's human nature. Because the huge dog moves slowly and deliberately, she presents the illusion of being easier to control. That little bounding pooch appears impossible to predict or control. And in fact, as I learned in conversation, the Newf is indeed amenable toward kids, allowing them to lead her about when she feels like it. (When she feels like lying there, she lies there, and nothing a kid can do will budge her.)

This distrust of rapidly moving objects extends to people also, very much so. It seems as though you can't anticipate well what they're likely to do. Sedate people seem easier to control, perhaps easier to live with. It's probably not true, of course. I'm talking about perceptions, not the reality. As a rule, however, as one person's nervous energy increases, so does the edginess of the people around him.

That's a powerful disadvantage for the ADD adult who must sway people in a sedate setting—a stock broker, for example, or a lawyer. For myself, I find that sometimes the hardest part of counseling people is simply to sit there. Activity can be a disadvantage in everyday social intercourse. You don't want to be annoying people and putting them on guard. You want to be liked. Nearly any human being does. Bouncing around like a Ping-Pong ball in tournament play doesn't do a thing for social situations.

Constant movement is particularly irritating to a non-ADD mate, who has to live in close proximity to it so much of the time. In fact, quite a number of dyed-in-the-wool hyperactives literally rock themselves to sleep in bed. Guess how well that goes over with a sleepmate.

Impulsivity offers its own set of disadvantages.

The natural human response when encountering a problem is fight or flight. The ADD adult will impulsively do one or the other—flare up in instant anger or immediately back away altogether. Too often, neither response is a good one. Let's take for example the ADD hyperactive who gets into a mild fender bender. To most people, this is an annoyance, an inconvenience, with the overriding thought looming that their insurance is going to go up. Bummer. Most folks sit down with the driver of the other car, morosely exchange several numbers, and go on their way.

The ADD hyperactive might blow up all out of proportion to the occasion, whether the bump was his fault or the other person's. I saw a young man do just that; the car ahead of him stopped for a red light and they locked bumpers. The kid jumped out of his car and literally threw a fit, yelling, kicking not just his tires but the door of his car as well. He did more damage than the collision did.

The hyperactive, on the other hand, might go into instant denial, either driving away as if nothing happened (legally a very dangerous thing to do) or hustling around with a fast, perfunctory meeting with the other driver, then getting on the road again. Either way, the hyperactive has shot himself in the foot, inflicting more damage on himself than the situation warrants.

Jeri makes this observation regarding my impulsivity, and she's right. "Sometimes Rick will jump into a discussion about a fairly sensitive topic with no thought that another time might be more appropriate. He just doesn't weigh his choice of words the way most people would.

"We used to experience this almost weekly on the way to Sunday morning church. We have a long drive in. Generally, by the time we got to church one of the children or I or all of us would be upset by something Rick had said. This couldn't go on. So we decided that we would really try to use the drive time as a time of meditation and praise, listening to good music and just enjoying each other's presence. It's made a great difference. Now we don't go to church all out of sorts and grumpy."

But there's a much greater danger than just some ruffled feelings. The impulsive's constant desire to move on to new things endangers the marriage relationship itself. Every relationship, and the marital bond in particular, has its extremes, its very highs and very lows. When life gets heavy, and irritations stack up, it's a real temptation to simply quit and move on. For the ADD adult driven by impulsivity and perhaps by hyperactivity as well, the friction can eventually outweigh the positives, and divorce looks a whole lot easier than does hanging in there.

Unfortunately, in some ways divorce is easier. Not better, of course. Certainly not! But easier. And an impulsive whose gut-level reaction is denial and escape might be overwhelmed by the desire to put yesterday behind. (Remember, that's easier for ADD adults than for most people. We really can forget the past.)

The non-ADD mate must remember when friction occurs

that long-range commitments are really, really hard for us. I don't suggest that the non-ADD spouse ought to give in when giving in is not appropriate or has to walk on eggshells to avoid confrontations or problems. I just want you to be aware of the reality.

Sometimes you can't fit the hyperactive into a slot; no good slot is available. Sometimes the ADD mate gets to fretting over what she perceives as excessive restrictions and irritations. And what about the non-ADD mate who tires of putting up with irritation? A line must be drawn, and the ADD adult and spouse can draw it one of three ways. One, they can learn to live with certain aspects of hyperactivity and impulsivity, and two, the ADD adult changes; or three, the non-ADD mate changes. It's so, so simple and so, so difficult.

The Solution

"Why should I fix myself? I'm not broke!" That's the not unreasonable cry of the ADD spouse. You hear it all the time. Society, and even counselors, are telling us ADD adults that we're not wrong, just different. Fine. So let us stay different.

But it's not that easy.

The first step in curbing unproductive, damaging hyperactivity and impulsivity is the ADD adult's awareness that change is desirable, even necessary. The proposed change is not desirable because something is broken and needs fixing. Rather it's because the activity level is causing problems. The ADD adults who are bouncing off walls are not going to achieve the goals they want, let alone stay out of trouble, unless some things change.

Know what turned me around, more than anything else? First Peter 3:7, where Peter instructs husbands to live considerately with their wives, bestowing honor upon them. Consideration. Honor. Driving the raisins right out of Jeri's oatmeal cookie wasn't exactly being considerate or honoring. I was frustrating the woman to whom I'd pledged my life. That embarrassed and shamed me. I was supposed to be taking care of her, not in a patronizing way, but as the husband, nurturing her as she nurtures me. Instead, I was turning her off and driving a wedge between us.

There are many motives for change, probably as many as there are hyperactive ADD adults. A juvenile corrections officer, wearied by years in the trenches, offered this reflection: "So often, the discipline we impose from the outside doesn't do a thing. The incorrigible juvenile ends up in the system as an incorrigible adult. But a few things work. The motive that works best can't be bottled; it happens now and then at random. That's love. The one thing that can turn a bad boy around is a good girl."

Commitment to Jesus Christ can provide the impetus to work past impulsivity and hyperactivity, particularly when the ADD adult realizes that Jesus needs a better diplomat than what that person is providing.

There are a variety of ways to manage hyperactivity and impulsivity. Sometimes a few simple changes do the trick. Other people need stronger tools. The harshest tools, so to speak, are drugs.

Drug Regimens

We give a variety of behavior-altering drugs to hyperactive kids. The process often works well enough that the child can settle down and start learning. Usually these drugs are discontinued as the person gets older. Most people assume that hyperactivity is a childhood problem that evaporates with maturity. And usually, as a person enters adulthood, improvement in some form occurs.

Some adults, however, profit from the continuation of drug therapy. Cylert works on some, and Ritalin has proved effective. Other drugs include Trofanil, Imiparine, and Dexadrine. Drug therapy is a last resort rather than the first course of action. Often, the ADD adult profits greatly simply by altering surroundings to an extent.

Environmental Changes

The environment we're considering here, of course, has little to do with rain forests. I'm talking about your immediate surroundings, where you work and live. Let me offer some suggestions for making adjustments in the workplace, because that's where most people spend the majority of their waking hours. Besides, a good work record with the possibility of advancement is an important goal. As you consider these suggestions, consider also how each step can be applied beyond the workplace, in the home setting, even on the road. The principles apply just about anywhere. In other words, although I'm talking about the work environment here, I want you to extend the ideas as far as you can, into your every environment.

Cocoon yourself.

A great curb to impulsivity, and to hyperactivity to a lesser extent, is simply to reduce stimuli. If the trigger's not pulled, the gun won't go off. Somehow, get a place to yourself where stimulation and disturbance will be minimal. Either wangle an office of your own or screen off a small cubicle in a corner.

In this separated space, keep visual stimuli to a minimum. That includes pictures on the wall (the blander the better, if they insist you decorate). Anything visible will catch your eye. If possible, everything in your space should be work-related.

Similarly, install a radio, a fan, a boom box or whatever to provide white noise. If your office plays a distracting style of music (vocal, for example, or country-western if you're a classical buff—whatever steals your attention and refuses to fade into the woodwork) over the PA system, get them to cut the speaker at your end.

When I'm reading Scripture, I absolutely need a place where, when I sit still, nothing is calling to me to get up and move again. Remember that distractions do far more than just rip attention away; they trigger activity and impulsive behavior also.

Let's pretend that you're an ADD male and your non-ADD

mate fancies Victorian decor. Now Victorian is as busy and elaborate as you can get, with silk tassels dangling everywhere you look. It might pay to sit down together, the two of you, and plan which rooms will belong to whom. Since we're pretending, we'll pretend the non-ADD wife yearns to do the living room up like a real Victorian parlor, and the kitchen—she sees a gas or electric stove cleverly concealed in a fake "wood-burning" Queen stove.

Good. Let her have the kitchen and her parlor. The bedroom, too, since the lights are going to be out when you use it anyway. (There's this four-poster bed . . .) But the family room, not the separate living room, has the fireplace. Turn the family room, therefore, into the Victorian parlor and close the living room off with a screening wall and door. You, the ADD mate, can now create for yourself a nonstimulating place to be. A few very plain (but comfortable) pieces of furniture, no pictures, no bric-a-brac or trophies, books in a cabinet with doors . . . work it out. This is not a "decorated" room as such. It's a place to unwind and to concentrate when concentration is essential.

Arrange your work space for *you*.

Do you prefer to work on the floor? Then stuff the desk up against the wall and make it a storage surface for files, piles of papers, and books. Use the kind of chair you do well in, or clear yourself floor space, if that's how you work best. Do you suppose someone might laugh or criticize? Let them, as you march up to get your merit promotion.

Work space management does not mean just an office area. It pertains anywhere. Shape it to your special needs. A carpenter acquaintance carries all his hand tools except his saws in a big pouch, like a manually adept kangaroo. "I used to see a need or problem, whip out some tool, and have at it. I'd put a nail where a screw should go because it was easier to pull the hammer out of a loop on my belt than to get the right screwdriver. My favorite saying was, 'So what? It got the job done.' That sure didn't score points with the customers. To slow me down and put the brakes on my impulsivity, I keep everything in one jumble now. By the time I dig out something to use, I've thought about the problem a few moments. That simple ten-second curb on my impulsivity has made me a better carpenter."

Is his approach unconventional? Sure. ADD adults are. Incidentally, this carpenter is over forty years old, and he's only been using his in-a-jumble system a couple of years. We're often slow learners. Had he thought about it and tried out various things, instead of expecting the world to adjust to his methods, he could have been a better carpenter years sooner.

The trick is to get past that first impulse. The second choice, whatever it is, is very frequently better.

Cater to your individuality.

You're different. It's expected that you'll employ different methods to achieve an end. Don't be shy about doing that. When the left-brain conventional world cries, "But that's not how you do it!" your reply is, "No, that's not how *you* do it."

For an example, let's take planning a complex project. Normally, this requires sitting down and doing a lot of brainstorming and arranging on paper. The hyperactive simply can't do that.

So get a deck of index cards and just start writing down the little sub-tasks in that major task as they come to you. At this stage, don't bother with sequence. The end. The beginning. The middle. It doesn't matter. Your mind does better with global thinking, so don't bother yet to track sequentially. Take cards with you as you do other things. This method fits right into the hyperactive's peripatetic lifestyle. You can be planning projects while you sit in line to get your car inspected, while you're picking up the kids after their soccer game, while you're eating breakfast—whenever the thoughts come. Pace back and forth. Note that you can write on index cards while you're pacing all the way to San Antonio, if you want.

Eventually, you will spread the cards out on the floor and arrange them sequentially into a time line or order of completion. Set yourself little mini-deadlines according to the cards, and put them on a calendar. You're on your way.

When planning lesser projects, write plenty of short breaks right into the work so you don't sit too long. You might want to tackle two projects simultaneously, one requiring activity and one sedentary, then switch between them. Two birds with one stone.

Impulsivity has scuttled many a worthy project. When an editor contracts for a book, the publishing house will probably require a complete manuscript from a beginning writer. The person who has already written half a dozen books need only phone the editor to discuss the project, and a contract is forthcoming. What's the difference? The experienced writer has proven himself. That person can stick with the project, seeing it through to completion. That person will not impulsively make a grand start with lots of promises and then never finish. The editor has no assurance that a beginning writer can complete the promised book. What looks great at the front end so very often bogs down before the finish.

There is an additional way to keep impulsivity from being that kind of a problem in your life. It also helps greatly in the matter of slowing down hyperactivity. Your success may require the service of a support person.

SUPPORT

Bet you were wondering when the non-ADD mate was going to show up in all this. Here it is. The non-ADD spouse can fill a major and necessary role in this channelling of hyperactivity and impulsivity. That person can serve as monitor to keep you from abandoning a project prematurely or leaping into some aspect of it too hastily. Other roles include encourager and advisor.

A friend I'll call John was notoriously slow about completing brief daily reports. But a coworker needed those daily reports.

His coworker was not averse, therefore, to literally standing on John's desk until the required report was completed. If John was exceptionally tardy, his coworker might stomp on the desktop. This person was, in a way, a strong support person for John, although not a particularly tactful one. The non-ADD spouse can do better.

These are the qualifications for a good support person:

- The person genuinely cares about you.
- The person will refrain from lecturing you about what you should do. In other words, the person is patient with your seemingly strange ways.
- The person knows you well enough that he will not accept excuses.
- The person understands your need to work in small increments and will encourage you in your completion of mini-tasks, without waiting for the completion of the whole project to hand out some praise.

To get the full benefit of your support person, first give that person blanket permission to badger you, nag you, set deadlines. Presumably, the person does not need your permission to praise and encourage you. That blanket permission gives you control of the person's role but not of the input that person will provide. It's rather like electing a district judge. You vote for her, but you can't influence her decisions (ideally, anyway).

Now, make your support person aware of the plan you've set up. Point out the schedule. Then agree together how you will report your progress to your support person on each segment of the project. Arrange how you will tell him when it's done. Perhaps you'll report verbally or check off the mini-task on the calendar. Whatever, that support person will monitor your achievement and encourage or make suggestions appropriately.

Using a spouse as the support person can strengthen your marriage immensely. You see, a non-ADD adult has terrible trouble understanding how life looks from an ADD mate's perspective. Walking through a major project in this way, as support, gives him insight he could never gain otherwise.

There is one source of support nobody seems to think about—our own dear old Uncle Sam. With ADD and ADHD (attention deficit with hyperactivity) recognized at last for what they are, adults can claim help in certain quarters from the ADA—the Americans with Disabilities Act. In place since 1992, the act requires certain employers, including governments, to adjust and adapt the workplace to accommodate disabled workers. While this concept begins with things like wheelchair accessibility and parking for the handicapped, it also includes modifications an ADD adult might need in the workplace. Hardly the bugbear some painted it, the act does much to improve a company's bottom line. Something as simple as a high desk at which the ADD worker can stand instead of having to sit could greatly improve that person's productivity. Screens or doors to reduce distractions, white noise sources—that can all come under the umbrella of the ADA. It's well worth looking into.

To this point I haven't really dealt with another major factor in the ADD adult's life. Here again, we react differently than do most people. That factor multiplies impulsivity and hyperactivity, not to mention other friction.

Stress.

ADDRESSING STRESS PROBLEMS

J eri speaks:
   When Rick gets stressed, it shows up as hyperactivity and negativity. It seldom produces the long-term bad effects it does for me because he gets it all out right away, dumps it on the floor and walks off. Talking and moving are how he dumps it. Later, he won't even remember what he got stressed out about.

Me? I usually end up with headaches and gastritis or insomnia. Rick seldom suffers any of those problems. I could use improvement in handling stress, and Rick presents a positive model to emulate.

I have learned to take his stress cues pretty well—to know when a stressful day has made him more negative and I am, therefore, not to take his mood personally. I've learned when to encourage him to talk and what kind of questions to ask. If we can talk while avoiding arguing, it's a great stress reducer for Rick. Especially if we can joke or laugh, his mood lightens.

Every once in a while, however, talking isn't it. I have to be sensitive enough to realize that. Fortunately, I seldom see him take stress out on me or the kids anymore.

Rick speaks:
There are two kinds of stress, and I wasn't any good at handling either of them. One kind is what the world does to you. A traffic accident that couldn't be avoided. A meteorite taking out your living room. Then there's the other kind, which you deliberately or inadvertently do to yourself. A richly deserved traffic ticket qualifies. So does agreeing to take on more work than you can comfortably handle. That kind of thing. Either kind, I would react in one of two ways, both equally detrimental.

Sometimes I would blow up. I'd rain all over the nearest guilty—or innocent—party. I'd space out even while I was blowing and then forget about it. It was over. Why dwell on it? Do you know what that would do to the person on the receiving end of my stormy tirade?

Warning: Don't get angry back at me. Then I *really* go ballistic. You see the pattern? Something would stress me out. I'd become furious with whomever was handy. That person, being either marginally responsible for my problem or not at all, would get mad because I was unjustly blaming him or her and come back at me. That would tip me off worse. And away we'd go.

Jeri, on the other hand, never said a word to me. She'd just stuff her own fury and be a nice Christian wife. Not only was that devastating to her, it was doing me no favors. You don't let an ADD adult's destructive behavior continue unchallenged, or it will never improve.

Sometimes I'd simply disengage. Tune out. Often, I still do, in fact. There are situations where you don't dare space out or daydream, and I would do it anyway. I was a menace to myself and others, thanks to the stress that touches us all. Of all the areas of my life that have needed change and improvement consistently through the years, stress and anger management have been the two most important. And the greatest of these is stress.

STRESS AND THE ADD ADULT

A friend of mine who is also an MK—his parents served the mission field in Africa—tells about walking toward his house late at night and hearing a man go running by, followed closely by the thunder of a charging hippopotamus. A hippo on the run constitutes major stress. Your car lying upside down in the ditch on an icy, snowy day, its little wheels pointing toward the sky and a puzzled look on its little radiator face, constitutes stress. Confronting the two hundred separate parts of a tricycle or swing set that has to be assembled? That's not stress, right?

Yes it is, to an ADD adult. Taking an important examination is stress. Being given three projects at work when you only have time for one or two is stress. Trying to juggle home duties and work duties and the kids and an ailing parent and church obligations and volunteer service is big time stress.

To the ADD adult, anything overwhelming is stressful. Note I didn't say "seems stressful." It *is*. The non-ADD mate doesn't always grasp that.

Neither does the non-ADD mate always appreciate how we deal with stress, particularly that which comes from encounters with life that seem so overwhelming. For one thing, we become less able to think clearly. We are less creative. We are addled. As a defense against the feeling of being engulfed, we tune out. Here is where our famous daydreaming kicks in. It's sort of like a safety vent that lets go under pressure. However, the pressure doesn't have to be very great at all.

A kid in school, faced with two pages of arithmetic, tunes out and daydreams. This is not a conscious act. In fact, the child really does want to complete the work. Tuning out is an automatic response, programmed in. Suddenly, time is up and the child hasn't done but half a page.

BEATING RECOGNIZED STRESSORS

Adults react like that as well. Take the case of a bright woman with ADD—call her Britt—who took her state realtor's licensing exam. She was certain she knew the material. She'd been working at the business for several years as an aide. She flunked royally. The examiner asked her why she hadn't finished the exam; she probably would have passed if she had answered all the questions. She'd simply tuned out.

Sometimes this tuning out manifests itself as selective memory. We don't have Alls-heimer's, we have Some-heimer's. Our subconscious self picks and chooses, remembering some things and dismissing others.

"You remembered your flying lesson and you remembered to pick up Chip at school. So why couldn't you remember the dry cleaning stop I asked you to make?"

I had it written down, too.

The non-ADD mate isn't going to be able to help much when the ADD spouse's brain kicks out of gear like that. The only things I can suggest are:

- Give orders and requests one or two at a time.
- Call us back to reality when we space out and then repeat what we missed, if appropriate.
- Help relieve the stress if possible. Take some of the load off.

It may be that the non-ADD spouse notices what's coming before the ADD adult does. Signs suggest that something is happening; the ADD partner becomes even more forgetful than usual, or more easily irritated, or she daydreams more. The non-ADD spouse may be able to head off the stressor or reduce it. This kind of intervention would have to be provided on a case-by-case basis, so to speak. I can't offer guidelines because there are no easy steps or rules.

The overreaching principle is for the ADD mate to give the non-ADD spouse permission to comment on her observations. The ADD adult has the responsibility then of responding to the spouse's comments in a positive way—accepting them, considering them at least, acting on them if necessary.

The ADD spouse, though, is the one to work hardest on this problem. Here are some stress combatants.

TAKE A BREAK

You can't always do it, but when you can, getting your mind on other things helps. At the Minirth Meier New Life Clinic, office hallways track in a ring around a central cluster of rooms. You can walk hallways all day, passing the same rooms repeatedly, without changing directions. Just getting out and doing that ring once or twice can ease my stress.

Exercise is a dandy stress reliever.

Britt might have helped herself by standing up beside her chair and stretching every half page or so. She would plan this in advance, of course. "When I reach item 4, I'll pause," she might say to herself.

BREAK IT DOWN

Britt might also have taken the exam in smaller increments. This solution would have helped the kid doing pages of arithmetic also. Look on it as a half-page assignment. Finish it. Do another half page. Then another.

Had Britt skimmed the test, as I suggest in the how-to-study section, it would have helped in two ways. One was the direct way, in which she answered the questions she was certain about, thus guaranteeing at least that many points. Indirectly, skimming the test and answering out of sequence keeps interest up. The ADD adult's brain loves to flit. She could have taken advantage of that. With things done here and there the test becomes less and less stressful all the time.

Minimize Other Stressors

Britt would have flunked even more dismally, were her three-year-old son along. Taking the test on a day when company was scheduled for that evening or when she needed to take the car in to have it worked on or some other intrusion of modern life, she would have done worse.

Britt passed on her second attempt by working on the above points and by reminding herself that if she flunked this one she'd just take it again. It wasn't the end of the world. (In other words, she was minimizing the stress of the test itself.) Those humorless old left-brained test-makers weren't going to win *her* war!

Britt's stressors were easily identifiable. You sort of expect them to be what they are. For the ADD adult, however, unidentified stressors can sneak around undercover, going undetected, and wreak real havoc.

Identifying Hidden Stressors

Because it's basically a left-brain world, most articles and books describing how to identify stress talk about the stress affecting left brainers. Just as ADD itself often goes unrecognized, so do some of the things that trouble ADD-affected individuals.

For example, for the ADD adult, routine and sameness actually become stressful after a while. We grow bored with the same old thing, day in and day out. Pretty soon, we get irritated. If the pressure of sameness and routine is not alleviated, we begin developing all the signs and symptoms of major stress. Suddenly, we're not much fun to be with, and all too often, no one realizes why.

The non-ADD adult is certainly not likely to understand what is happening (neither does the ADD adult, usually). After all, most non-ADD adults find comfort and security in routine. "The rest of the world may spin right off its axis, but I'll be okay if I can just have my coffee and paper first thing." Very frequently, in fact, non-ADD adults take refuge from stress by burying themselves in routine. Of course they're not going to recognize the ADD mate's problem.

A similar unseen stressor is workload. What seems about right to the left brainer may be overwhelming to the ADD adult. The ADD adult, however, grew up with the "wisdom" that if only he applies himself better, he can handle it. Therefore, his workload must not be unbearably heavy. Chances are, it's bearable, but at a heavy cost of stress.

Unavoidable annoyances can produce stress signs and symptoms also. Let's take as an example a young man with ADD trying to get ahead as a television reporter. That's a stressful occupation. He's called out on assignments at odd hours and is required to acquit himself well in emergencies and other sudden, unexpected situations. Let's also say that he gets the dirt patrol—the police blotter, the ugly accidents. He sees murders, fatal crashes, and innocent children scarred by brutal forces.

A left brainer would say that the stress in that young man's life comes from the irregular work hours, the nastiness of what he confronts and reports upon almost daily (victims' blood and guts can take a heavy toll on emergency personnel and others), and the pressure of instantaneous, high-profile decisions. What he must decide on the spur of the moment can come back to haunt him years later when someone decides to sue, or a criminal goes free because he too eagerly reported details that should have remained secret. He sees a great story get spiked for petty or even sinister reasons.

So much for what the left brainer knows. In reality, it's not at all like that. Because of his short attention, the young man can probably handle ugliness surprisingly well. He can put the images and aftermath of mayhem behind him without much trouble. He deals with the lack of routine with aplomb; routine is anathema to him. He doesn't mind the pressure of an instantaneous decision a bit; he functions well on instant-ness, on spur-of-the-moment. He can go for the jugular in a reporting situation because he doesn't give a rip about the possibility of a lawsuit three years from now. In many regards, he's perfect for the job, and he does it well.

The pressure he feels is the need to appear as something he often is not—crisp, rested, well-attired, and nattily groomed in *every* situation. He hates having to have his hair combed simply because others think it ought to be. He doesn't like pretense, and often a television reporter must present a false personal image. He feels the stress of having to clear an assignment he believes is immensely important with a news director he may or may not (if he's ADD, probably not) get along with. He has to be nice to a lot of people he can't stand, and the hypocrisy really gets to him.

The left-brain news director may say with all sincerity, "The pressure is getting to this guy. Let's give him the entertainment beat. Regular hours. He can interview celebrities who come through, review restaurants and shows, pick up the color stuff, make himself useful around the front newsroom." The woman, in her ignorance, has just cancelled out the young man's strengths, but the stressors are all still in place—intensified, in fact, now that he's on a nine-to-five shift. He still has to be hypocritical in his dealings with people, has to present a certain stereotypical appearance that isn't really him, and now he sees breaking news go right by him while he dings around with things that don't interest him. The news director is about to lose a promising employee.

How do you recognize the real stressors in a situation, when the prevailing left-brain wisdom thinks they are all neatly identified? Here's where the non-ADD spouse and ADD adult put heads together to work out the truth.

Let's use as an example not just the young man in the illustration above but also you. What are the stressors in his life and yours?

Sit down with the non-ADD mate, or with another non-ADD person who knows you well and cares about you. Don't just answer the following questions. Brainstorm them. Talk about them. Lead each other into insights. The questions are framed to target the ADD adult.

1. What is it you most of all do *not* look forward to as your day begins? Be specific. As the chores of the day loom before you, what do you dread most having to take care of?
2. Similarly, what do you dread most about weekends and/or other days off?
3. Expand the above two questions by asking, "Okay, what else bugs me at work and off duty?"
4. Identify what you like most about the average day at work and the average off-duty day.
5. What else do you like about your days on and off?
6. List the last five things to have really bugged you. Are those things happening over and over or only occasionally?
7. What has your non-ADD spouse noticed in this regard? What has he or she seen as stressors in your life, no matter how unpredicted or unusual according to conventional wisdom?
8. If you have kids, ask them when they notice that you seem upset or stressed out or irritable. Relationships mean everything to kids. As a result, they are often extremely observant and insightful regarding changes in mood and relationship.
9. Knowing what you know now about yourself and your ADD tendencies, what aspects of your life run counter to ADD propensities? For instance, you know ADD people are spontaneous. In what ways is spontaneity squelched in your life?
10. If your life were perfect, what would be different about your normal working day? Your normal off-duty day?

In-depth discussion of these ten questions should reveal some irritants in your life. Most irritants are merely that—irritants. But those irritants could well be cleverly-masked stressors also. They may also point to the stressors indirectly. For example, the television reporter learned that he hated getting dressed for work. Power colors, white shirt, correct tie. He hated spending time at the barber's every single week. He loved weekends in blue jeans or cutoffs.

Those irritants pointed to his root problem of having to present what he thought was a hypocritical appearance. But he and his mate had to really drum with the band to come up with it.

Review with your spouse what you came up with. Exp¹ re possible underlying meanings for these observations. What root causes might be playing an undercover stress role in your life?

That was the fun part. Now you have to figure out how to reduce the stress. Again, brainstorming may bring workable answers. ADD adults are very good at brainstorming because of that gift for thinking globally. The non-ADD mate with the linear thinking is very good at working out a practical application. You need each other on this.

The TV reporter reduced his stress level considerably by asking for and receiving a change in the line of command he followed. Rather than dealing directly with his news director, he worked through the female anchor, who was also mildly ADD. The anchor understood him better than did the director, but the two women, anchor and director, worked well together. With the buffer of an understanding person between him and a major, though unintentional, irritant, they all functioned better.

He also struck a deal with his on-site cameraman. He would be taped from the waist up only. So here he appeared at the scene of the newsbreak, reporting up a storm, his necktie in place—and his jeans or cutoffs safely out of frame. The shirt and tie came off as soon as the bite was wrapped, and he'd revert to a sweatshirt.

In his case an interesting fringe benefit developed that he had not expected. His informal attire off camera permitted him to get in close to people who would have clammed up for a guy in a suit. He interviewed bartenders, street people, drug dealers, an informative array of neo-hippies—and he loved it! His enthusiasm for his job improved immeasurably just because of the new variety in it.

Look for your unidentified stressors. Dig 'em out! Vanquish or modify them as you are able! Perhaps like that reporter you will find renewed joy and enthusiasm as a result.

Sometimes dealing with stressors requires backing away from them. The prevailing left-brain wisdom requires that you confront problems rather than run from them. That is true, in some regards. However, the left-brain world often feels that any change or shift constitutes running away. For the ADD adult, that's not always so. We more than most people can often profit greatly from change. Don't let a left brainer tell you that you have to face the problem head-on. There may be a better way.

In fact, a change of scene, whether it may be construed as running away or not, is often what the doctor would order for the right-brained stressee.

CHANGING THE SCENE

When I started the Minirth Meier satellite clinic in Longview, Texas, I was flying high! We got the clinic up and running, and before long I was seeing forty clients a week. That's a heavy workload, for it's not just a matter of interacting with each client for the allotted hour. Besides the counseling session itself, there is an immense amount of outside work involved with each client as well; research, study, paperwork, assessment. In addition, there would be emergency sessions when someone would crash and burn emotionally and need immediate help.

That all lasted about two years. ADD adults burn out more easily than do most people. I won't call it boredom. It's not that exactly. It's more a restlessness, a dissatisfaction with the present situation. I hung in with it, but the job I once loved was becoming a stressful burden.

Then they asked me to come to Dallas to become part of the administrative team. In addition, I would be expected to conduct seminars and write. That job change has made all the difference!

The variety gets me past those spates of dissatisfaction. When I become burned out on one aspect, I can shift to another. My enthusiasm has remained high for the years I've spent in what is essentially one position.

Moves and changes are not necessarily a cure-all. They exact a price, and it is often the non-ADD spouse who pays.

KEEPING STRESS REDUCTION IN PERSPECTIVE

Because totally different stress factors produce totally different results in the lives of right brainers as opposed to left brainers, one person's meat becomes the other's poison. That must never be allowed to happen in the marriage relationship.

The non-ADD mate may complain about the ADD spouse's fleeting interest, easy burnout, and frequent desire to move on. Constant shifts are as unnerving to some non-ADD mates as surprises are to ADD adults. Let's pretend for the moment that in my case Jeri did not want to move from Longview to the Dallas area (not true; it's just a what-if). What could she have done?

ALWAYS CONSIDER THE SPOUSE

Considering the needs and preferences of others is awfully hard sometimes for the ADD mate to do. We get all wrapped up in our thrill of the moment and forget everything else. How many, many times I've fallen down in this regard! The ADD mate should flawlessly observe two rules of thumb: no major decisions without spousal approval, and no major decisions without a brainstorming session.

The first rule does not mean, "No major decisions without perfunctory spousal approval," or ". . . spousal rubber-stamp." Jeri ought not expect me to come sweeping through the door with a cheery, "Hi, Honey. I'm selling the house. That's okay, isn't it?" (Don't laugh; I've done it.) That's expecting a rubber-stamp approval, assuming I think forward enough to mention it to her at all. I've done some pretty major things without remembering to tell Jeri, like buying cars, boats, and houses.

The second rule insures that the first will be thoroughly observed. A brainstorming session provides enough time for a hesitant or reticent non-ADD spouse to express himself or herself and to offer needed input. By their very nature, major decisions have to be scrutinized closely, and ADD adults just don't do that. The ADD adult must recognize the value of the mate's point of view.

This is not to say that the ADD spouse automatically bends to the non-ADD mate's wishes. Not at all. There are times I appreciate Jeri's position, but I want to do it my way anyhow. But I had better know what her views are and weigh them against my own.

In considering the mate's needs and preferences, it's wise to uncover the options available in any decision.

There Are Always Options

The ultimate goal is to find some measure of contentment for both partners. In the matter of the move from Longview, Jeri could have sat down with me and together we would brainstorm options. If I took a particular course of action, how would she feel? If she had to do follow-through on this decision, what would make her feel better about it? What options might I have for staying in Longview and liking it? An example might be for me to get more into the administrative aspects of the branch clinic. We would put the best possible spin on the situation and come to some sort of agreement. Or truce. Whatever.

A word of warning here: such brainstorming sessions, when each partner holds vigorously to an opposing point of view, can easily turn into shouting matches. Know that anger is hanging just above your shoulder every moment. These are emotional issues, even the most innocuous of them.

Before you start discussion of the topic at hand (e.g., "Shall we move?"), therefore, lay some ground rules for avoiding acrimony. Here's one suggestion: get a role of uncoated, unwaxed shelf paper and pencils, pens, or crayons (ideally, a different color for each spouse). Insist from the beginning that both partners jot down a couple of reminder words every time they speak. Start at the beginning of the roll and continue on down nonstop during the course of the discussion.

This keeps the ADD mate focused. It helps prevent him or her from going off half-cocked and from missing the other person's point. If I have to write down several words every time I speak, I'll hesitate, and in hesitating I might hear more. The non-ADD mate can see the progress and hear better also.

You can still use the paper, afterward, to line the cabinet shelves.

There is one source of stress that we have not dealt with as yet, and that's the kids, particularly ADD kids in the family. ADD adults and ADD kids tend to blow up more, rub each other more, and at the same time understand each other better. Kids. There are ways to handle that stress source also.

TEN

ADDolescents and Other Kids

J eri speaks:
   Our son Chip, an ADD kid, is in his teens now. He's
an amazing mix of little and big, young and old, mature
and goofy. You should hear his deep, gravelly telephone voice.
He sounds like Darth Vader without the menace. He's great at
games and stunts, and you'd think he hasn't a serious bone in
his body. And yet you can trust him to think clearly in an
unusual situation.

There are weeks when it seems as though we are on Chip
constantly about chores, and neatness, and schoolwork. Chip
knows his ADD makes him forgetful, so he generally takes our
chiding pretty good-naturedly. I feel sorry about it anyway.

The more I work with Chip, the more I understand Rick.
And the better I understand Rick and his ADD, the easier it is
to work with Chip. That's both good and bad. Because they
are so much alike, their relationship tends to be a little stormier
than some. I end up refereeing from time to time. And yet, Rick

has a modifying effect on me as well. When I get frustrated with some aspect of Chip's nature or personality, Rick brings me back to reality. That reality is that Chip is Chip.

And he's a marvelous Chip.

Rick speaks:

Dealing with Chip and helping him grow well has been a real educational experience for me in several ways.

For one, I see him hit some wall that I hit when I was a kid. I know how painful it feels. But I see him respond to it differently from the way I did at his age. Usually, his way is better. I'm proud of him and happy for him. But there's a sense of jealousy, too, I guess you'd call it. I wish I could have known when I was a kid what I know now. My life would have been much less frustrating—different, as Chip's is.

The other educational experience laps over into my practice. As I learn better and better how to work with Chip and help him, I find principles and techniques that can help others with ADD problems. Even myself. I'm certainly not using Chip as a guinea pig—you know, the "Let's try this out on the kid and see if it works" approach—but he does provide valuable insights.

In fact, until Chip came along, neither Jeri nor I fully grasped the misery ADD was bringing to our marriage. He was an eye-opener, and we are eternally grateful to him.

Growing Up Different

Times have changed for the better as far as we right brainers are concerned. Back in the beginning of my college basketball days, the game was designed for left-brain athletes. Players had to memorize a playbook full of rigid plays with carefully rehearsed responses. If the opposing team's small forward did this, you did that. If your team was headed for the basket, you executed play number such and such. Very structured.

Ah, but an inordinate percentage of good team prospects—the guys who could really play B-ball—have been right brainers.

We don't do well memorizing plays and sticking to a rigid structure, but boy, can we tuck that old round thing into the hoop! And that's what counts.

In the last few years, therefore, basketball has opened up into virtually a new game, shifting essentially from left-brain strategies to right, with nifty passes, spontaneity, daring plays, and the full-court press. Right brainers, incidentally, tend to be notoriously poor at free throwing. Free throws require a lot of monotonous practice, a lot of concentration, a lot of precision. That's not the right brainer's way. We're better at the slam-dunk, the fast shot from outside, the innovative response to an unusual situation.

Curiously, a goodly percentage of athletes, prison inmates, and law enforcement officers are strongly right-brain. Many ADD adults are counted in that lot. All, each in his or her way, are strongly disciplined either from within or from without. Interestingly, all have chosen high-risk occupations. Right-brain people, and ADD adults in particular, don't mind living on the edge, taking chances.

What makes the difference between the life choices a prison inmate makes and a professional athlete? Between a con's and a cop's? Values.

When do they receive their values? Growing up.

Because of the pressure the outside world places upon them, ADD kids sense they are different, whether they consciously realize it or not. They're told to behave and develop one way; they behave and develop another, and they can't help it. They're given to know that they are different, and almost always given to know that they are wrong. This is a tough environment in which to grow positive values and a strong sense of confidence.

Here again, you're trying to grow grass in sand. From the seedling to a firm turf, you and your ADD child both need years of special attention. There are ways to provide plenty of extra water—praise—since he or she dries out quickly in the heat of criticism. Plenty of nourishment—both education and love—because the loose soil lets love and learning dissipate. Protection from the worst of the slings and arrows of life, for the soft soil allows root damage so easily. And the deeper your child's roots go, the happier he or she will be.

The ADD Adult as Parent

The parents of an ADD child, particularly a parent who is also ADD, must meet two challenges as they raise their little ones. One will be to discover things about themselves and use those discoveries to make their own lives richer and easier even as they are guiding their children. After all, the best sermon a child can hear is the parents' day-to-day living. The second challenge, of course, is to implant values and self-confidence when such planting is so very difficult.

This is particularly difficult for a non-ADD parent to accomplish. Non-ADD parents remember their own youth, remember all the other kids they grew up with, and like any other adult, they use those memories as a guide when raising the child. They remember how kids who did not pay attention—hyperactives especially—were blamed and admonished. They remember how those children were considered obstinate and difficult because of their deliberate desire to disobey. Worst of all, the non-ADD adult has no idea what is going on inside the ADD child's head.

In this chapter I'd like to do two things. Most of all, I want to educate the non-ADD adult on what is happening in an ADD child's life. This is an alien world to the grown-up. And of course, I also want to suggest ways in which the non-ADD adult can help the child learn and grow.

Ideally, the non-ADD adult and the ADD partner balance each other, each providing the insights of which the other is a bit short. Real life never works that way, but it's a worthy target.

Believe me, it can be terribly frustrating for a non-ADD parent to raise, essentially, two ADD kids, the spouse and the youngster. Multiply "are you listening?" by two. But the rewards and sense of accomplishment multiply as well.

In the course of raising an ADD child, the ADD parent will

grow as well. I see it in my life, I see it in the lives of others. Therefore, let us assume from here on out that we are talking about one child, the offspring of one ADD parent and one non-ADD parent. Actual family dynamics are always far more complex than that, of course. But this assumption will do for dealing with basic principles.

There are practical steps to take. One of the best ways to grow grass in sand then is to teach the child how to handle day-to-day skills in this left-brain world. Related to that is a need to teach the child how to improve responsibility. We do that by allowing appropriate control. Third, we must teach the child self-worth, knowing the child will perceive his or her differences as failures, and those perceived failures will certainly undermine self-esteem. The end, the overriding goal, is to teach wholeness—a respect, including the child's self-respect, for the child's differences.

These lessons must be ingrained in the ADD parent as well, and probably at the same time. ADD adults have what might be called a truncated maturity; we don't mature as thoroughly or as quickly as most people. We fall victim to childish thinking and acting all too frequently. So this learning process for kids and adolescents is equally valid for adults. The guide and administrator of the learning process usually is the non-ADD adult. And the ADD adult must give the non-ADD mate permission to function in that capacity. *Must!*

Let's take all the various aspects of this learning in order.

PAY ATTENTION TO YOUR RESPONSES

We ADD adults tend to respond to our children's behavior in one of two opposite ways. One, we remember what it was like when we were growing up, and we empathize with the little one. Or as we see the little one do something we disliked in ourselves or were chided for in our own childhood, we react negatively, maybe even angrily. We don't like seeing that part of ourselves relived. Too often, the ADD adult responds in the latter way.

Meanwhile, the non-ADD adult is responding pretty much to some inner vision of what he thinks the child ought to be doing—listening better, paying attention, or whatever. The non-ADD parent has a definite plan and appearance in mind for that child, and when the child doesn't reflect the image, trouble follows.

When I see Chip's irresponsibility in some area of his life, I see mine; not a pretty sight. It angers me. Since irresponsibility angers left brainers also, Jeri gets fried as well. Poor Chip, who didn't mean to be irresponsible and wishes he weren't, gets cut down in a withering cross fire.

You're not going to recognize the underlying reasons for your responses in the heat of the moment, at the time you are making them. Neither ADD nor non-ADD parents are that cool and sharp. So may I suggest that after a blow-up or an admonishment, when the thunder and lightning are done, think about why it occurred. Look back. The non-ADD parent can ask herself: What was I expecting of the situation, and can an ADD child actually deliver on that expectation? The ADD parent can ask: Was my kid's behavior a reflection of my behavior at that age? Does that bother me?

After both you and your child have simmered down, bring it up. Explain your insight. You need not apologize for being the way you are, but do ask forgiveness if any unfairness occurred. You will quite possibly blow it again the next time, but both you and your child will recognize what's going on and understand that human nature is at work here. That in itself will soften the blow of criticism. Seeing what's happening becomes progressively easier as you both mature. And you'll both feel better.

The ADD parent also has to keep in mind the child's attitude toward life; too many adults don't think of that.

Promote Practical Goals

Most goals set in this world are set by left brainers. I'm certain of it. They see thirty years down the road and adjust their lives accordingly. They can shape their whole lives by forces that the ADD youngster can neither recognize nor envision. ADD kids need immediate goals, and the non-ADD parents must understand that.

When I was growing up, it didn't do much good to tell me to shape up so I could be an outstanding citizen of the community. That desirable end was too far in the future to be on my priority list.

Staying out of trouble sure was, though. And that's a worthy goal for any person. There are times, of course, when adherence to principles is more important than steering clear of problems. I'm not talking about failing to stand up for what is right—that kind of trouble. I'm talking about the day-by-day irritations and chastisement that are so much a part of the ADD person's life.

By developing skills to appear more responsible, to discharge duties, to master impulsivity, the ADD child and adult avoid trouble with the left-brain world. There's the motivation to place before a youngster. It provides an immediate reward, the only kind of reward an ADD person really appreciates.

The motive to live as Jesus would have you live is an excellent one, but again, it is awfully vague for an ADD person to remember and follow. I like to think I'm better about employing that motivation now; Jeri says I very much am, but that came from long, slow growth through adulthood. I'm not sure I could consistently sustain that kind of motivation in youth. It is a worthy ultimate goal, therefore, but not necessarily an immediate working goal.

Another useful immediate attitude, the same as was mentioned in study habits, is to see life as a game. You against the world. As children get into school, age six or seven, they become very competitive. This is necessary as the children begin the process of separating their identity from their parents' and other kids'. That need to compete serves just as well as does the desire to stay clear of blame and trouble. Together, they provide the child with powerful and near-instantaneous incentives to learn.

The non-ADD parent here acts as a tempering influence; a

kid can get carried away treating life as a game. The non-ADD parent then will walk a tightrope between allowing a carefree attitude and helping the ADD adult and child hew to responsibility.

Keep the goals immediate. Keep them relevant. Eventually the ADD child will mature into the kind of person who reflects well upon his or her Lord, and that's the ultimate goal.

Maturity involves discipline, and ADD adults tend to have problems with discipline duties.

Keep Discipline Consistent

An ADD adult is not the world's greatest disciplinarian. We often blow up and overreact. Anger leaps in instantly and rakes the kid over the coals for what, if you stopped and thought about it, was a minor infraction.

Or we fail to notice the infraction and therefore don't act at all. The kid gets away with murder because the ADD adult isn't thinking about the child's actions. This is particularly damaging to the child if the other parent *does* notice. Parents have to be in absolute agreement on what constitutes an infraction, as well as what happens when it occurs.

Or we ADD parents inappropriately mix the disciplinary measure with a cheerful "Fuss? What fuss?" attitude. In this case we've just castigated our kid for some misbehavior, the child is angry and fearful, and we start acting like nothing bad ever happened. You see, the ADD parent quickly dismisses that kind of thing. A non-ADD child stews a while. An ADD child will probably forget quickly about the fuss also.

How do you keep that kind of uneven, topsy-turvy, ineffectual discipline to a minimum? There are a few things you should try, and in all of them the non-ADD parent plays a central role. One of the easiest is simply to back off.

Get out of there.

Often, the ADD adult is not the appropriate person to administer discipline. Call in reinforcements, the non-ADD parent if possible. A trusted neighbor if necessary. But don't handle the situation yourself *unless*—and this is a very big unless—you have yourself well in control. Have you thoughtfully and carefully considered the problem? Can you speak calmly and with wisdom? If not, present your side of the case and let another person take over. Afterward, when the dust has settled, explain to the child, even a small child, that you feel the kid would get a better shake from a third party. The child will interpret that as "getting off easier." Your meaning is, "You escaped death, kid."

You see the non-ADD parent's role here. Mediator. Advocate. Enforcer. But the non-ADD parent has another task, and it's not an easy one: to understand and forgive the volatility. Instead of saying, "What's the matter with you? You're making a fool of yourself, overreacting like that!" which is inflammatory to say the least, how about, "Whoa! I see what's happening and I'll explain later. You promised to back off if I asked you to. I'm asking. Back off."

When problems crop up and you the ADD parent later realize what happened, apology is always appropriate. Not easy. Appropriate.

Make yourself apologize for overreactions.

Hard to do. It's done later, after the fact, after you've realized there would have been a better way. But do it. This is not something the non-ADD parent can help out with. You blew it; you apologize.

Also, keep the parenting team a team by bringing in the other member regularly.

Give the non-ADD mate blanket permission to help.

"Help" runs the gamut from neutral observation to strong interference. The non-ADD mate should have your permission ahead of time to insert himself into a situation and bring balance to your reaction, whether it be overdone or underdone. A buffer.

ADDolescents and Other Kids **179**

The non-ADD mate might say, "You gave me permission to interfere here, and right now, I think you're treating Junior too harshly." Or "You asked me to speak up when you failed to see a problem. I bring to your attention Junior's disobedience." Incidentally, the non-ADD mate ought do this *in private* as much as possible.

That way, especially when he's all worked up over some situation, the ADD parent doesn't get the knee-jerk feeling that his spouse is taking control away from him. He has already given his spouse control, which actually puts *him* in ultimate control. That doesn't seem important to non-ADD mates; it's incredibly important to ADD parents.

Often, the ADD adult and non-ADD mate think at right angles to each other, it seems. That's an important fact of life which both parents must keep in mind, for it constantly colors and shapes parental interaction with children. Jeri and I sure do. What I think is okay behavior she objects to. And what she feels is important—a regular bedtime, for example, I tend to treat pretty cavalierly.

So Jeri and I have to agree on working rules of the house. We don't work this out in front of the kids, either. We keep it behind closed doors. Each of us gives in on some points. We write down our compromise conclusions. We both agree to enforce the degree of discipline we've agreed upon and not the discipline we like better.

In short, we're not going to undercut each other. We're not going to cancel each other's desires out. The kids are going to meet a solid, united front. When Dad says this is the way it is, so does Mom. When Mom says this is how it is, Dad's voice is added to it. If Dad corrects a particular behavior, so does Mom, whether Mom feels like it or not, and vice versa. You'd be amazed how much difference this simple concept of being in agreement can make.

You cannot assume the child sees and appreciates all this effort on her behalf. You have to tell her of your affection.

Reassure and Reaffirm the Child Constantly

Reassure constantly! This need is particularly true for the non-ADD parent, who is likely to bump heads with an ADD child often.

Any child needs affirmation. Remember, however, that we ADD folk are the same as everyone else only much more so. If the child has ADD, you have to remind him or her over and over and over *ad nauseam:* "Your worth is determined not by behavior or grades but by who you are—our kid, God's child."

Make certain your child knows you are there for him, and then make equally certain you *are* there. You will not lie, cheat, or fulminate on the child's behalf, but you will surely support. You'll not turn on the child. You'll not automatically side with the teacher or some other outsider (neither will you pull the rug out from under a teacher's sincere efforts). Your love will not falter.

Jeri says, "I can give Chip a dozen positive strokes, but he'll recall the negative one he got yesterday. It's terribly hard for me to realize how attuned to criticism ADD kids are—any kids are, but ADD kids are especially. And there are times I have to criticize and correct. So I do it with as much of a positive spin as possible. I try to make even the correction affirming."

Also, for maximum effectiveness as parents, both of you must pay attention to what is going on in your family's corporate life. When so many forces tug at the day, it's easy to forget the special dynamics of an ADD-tinged family and grow impatient.

Pay Attention to What's Happening

Because the tendency to ADD can be inherited, as are so many other physical and physiological differences among human beings, the ADD adult may well end up with one or more kids showing signs of ADD. For example, our son does; our daughter does not.

It's very easy for the non-ADD adult to fall into the left-brain mind-set of, "If you can't learn, you're lazy or it's otherwise your fault somehow." Patience wears thin for any parent sometimes. The ADD parent, therefore, is the Great Reality Check of the family. "Wait a minute! Let's approach our child's [lack of attention], [forgetfulness], [whatever] differently!" The ADD parent is in the perfect position to see when the child needs something better than a left-brain approach and to promote alternatives.

This is hard for the non-ADD adult to accept, because the concept that left-brain attributes are the "right" attributes have been drilled into that person a whole life long.

There are a few aspects to parenting to which the ADD parent ought pay special attention. One of them is the model that parent offers any child.

Set an Example

The ADD parent who wants to teach an ADD child how to smooth the way through life had better be learning those skills himself or herself. Nothing helps the child learn these lessons better than seeing the parent succeed. Children are imitators. The ADD parent's best means of teaching, then, is to improve those skills and let the child see them in action.

The non-ADD parent can serve very well in several ways. One way is by pointing out the ADD parent's success in a positive context.

"Your dad writes down things he has to do the minute he hears about them, and it really helps him stay on course. Let's get you a notebook so you can do that."

"Your mom figures out a menu for the week so that she can do grocery shopping more efficiently. That same method will work when you're figuring out what supplies to get for school. Let's sit down and make a list. What subjects do you have this year?"

Another way the non-ADD parent can assist the ADD parent is by avoiding criticism of ADD-induced habits and characteristics. Making unkind comments is tantamount to biting each other. The two parents are teammates together in a no-holds-barred fight. *Fight* is not too strong a word. It's a constant battle these days to raise a child well in the world we live in. Keeping that child safe, teaching moral values and basic skills, has become increasingly difficult. It's a war out there that has entered every home. We as parents cannot afford to bicker with each other. We must present a strong, united front against powers far bigger and more insidious than ourselves.

Besides, when the non-ADD parent refers to the ADD parent's lacks (such as impulsivity, difficulties remembering, and such) as shortcomings, the kid picks up on that in an instant. ADD people are great at seeing and seizing negativity. "Daddy forgot the milk and Mommy is mad. Forgetting is bad, and I forget a lot." The last thing you want is for the child to feel he or she is the hopeless victim of ADD, disliked by the non-ADD parent.

All this effective parenting is dependent upon good solid interpersonal relationships between the family members.

BUILD REAL RELATIONSHIPS

We ADD adults tend to put schedules and nooses and too-tight neckties in pretty much the same category. Here's a place, though, where scheduling ought to be. That's to set aside specific, exclusive time for the kids. Each child gets you for a while every week, at least. The family as a unit gets you for so many hours a week.

Just how much time you spend in this is up to each person on a case-by-case basis. But the only way you will build a relationship with a child is to spend time with her. Don't divide it into quality time and garbage time. It's all time. Take the kids along to the store, to the library, to the post office. Go along with the kids to soccer practice, to the playground, to the movies. Watch videos together. Find neat stuff, action stuff, to do together. Most of all: Listen. Listen. Listen.

And, of course, as long as you follow those general guidelines, life will be roses and birds singing.

When pigs fly.

Ah, wouldn't it be great if a few neat precepts could protect us from hard times! The ADD parent, even when well-yoked with a non-ADD parent, is going to hit rough stuff. Life doesn't go smoothly for left brainers; it goes even worse for righties. Here there are no rules that work across the board, but there are some useful guidelines.

Managing the Rough Times

Rough times happen in various ways. The kids generate some themselves. You get some serious backlash from your kids when your opinion of what's going to happen and theirs differ. You may not be doing what they want; they may not be doing what you want.

This sort of friction usually reaches a boiling point around age twelve or thirteen. That's when the child is perfecting a personal identity apart from the family's, and that means they have to separate themselves from the family. Distance themselves. They do that by opposing and resisting.

No one feels the heat of that friction more than does the non-ADD parent. There's a tendency to friction there anyway. The ADD child does not seem to be maturing and taking responsibility nearly as quickly or as well as the non-ADD parent thinks he or she should. Frustration flares.

Friction, in other words, is going to happen. There are some ways to minimize it, however. One of the best ways is to give the child permission to express feelings and needs.

Allow the Child a Voice

This is especially important when an ADD teen is approaching adulthood. Older children need a voice in their destiny but not necessarily a voice in the final decisions. What you're offering is their input into your process of making a major decision on their behalf. The child who can express needs and wants, who knows that her opinion is heard and valued (regardless whether it is honored by action or not), is far less likely to generate excessive friction.

Be aware that teens given the platform to express themselves will lobby heavily. It's up to you, more so the non-ADD parent, to keep a balance between allowing them whatever they argue for and denying them any say whatsoever. Help them make responsible choices. And by all means, value the child's opinion.

However, the ADD adult often gets so wrapped up in what's going on at the verbal level that he or she misses the real meat of the child's message, the underlying meanings. ADD adults aren't real hot on grasping underlying meanings anyway. That lack leads to intense friction at times.

Don't Be Blind to Deeper Issues

Kids who pitch for one thing may actually be attempting to gain some other objective. They may not even be aware they're doing it. Don't respond just to the identified issue. What else is going on here? Are there problems, and what choices will cure which problems, if at all? What is in the best interest of the child?

Let's say you've made your decision, and it's pretty close to the thing the child was asking for, but the kid isn't satisfied. You tried to be accommodating, but the child isn't buying your generosity. Chances are, the child had some underlying need or desire that your decision failed to satisfy. You feel as if you've lost twice over, and you don't even know why. What does the ADD adult, who has little or no luck with mysteries such as what goes on in kids' minds, do next? I suggest considering these points, and then going with it, whatever "it" is.

Make sure you've taken the best course for the child.

Confer closely with your spouse. Generally speaking (very generally; exceptions abound), the non-ADD mate is going to be better at grasping underlying or unspoken motivations. That parent can be a real help here. Agree on the decision or a variant of the original decision. Weigh it from whatever you know of the child's point of view and in the light of the child's welfare. Then stand by it.

Give kids permission to be angry.

You may be upset, the teen may be upset, but that's still the decision we go with. It's best. Don't expect the child to knuckle under with a false display of liking it. This sits especially poorly with ADD kids. You wouldn't do it yourself. So don't chastise a child for being angry.

Try to keep the lines of communication open.

This may require using a mediator other than the non-ADD parent. Be advised that as kids enter their teens, part of their separation involves attaching to a respected adult outside your home. A teacher, a youth leader, a neighbor becomes the adult-who-can-do-no-wrong, the trusted advisor. The child will believe that person when he rejects the exact same messages coming from his parents. That person may be the line of communication you end up using. But keep at least one line open.

Another rough issue can be school. And how! A single rough year is destructive for kids, any kids, but especially ADD kids. They're not absorbing the material rapidly to start with, and lost ground is awfully hard to regain. An entire rough school experience is devastating. For years, school is virtually the child's whole life. It will certainly govern the child's life to a great extent.

Monitor School Closely

Monitoring school means monitoring the child. What do you gauge? I'd keep an eye on the general tenor of the child's world—enthusiasm for life, general good spirits, lively interest in a variety of things, and occasional obsessions with a particular thing—dinosaurs, castles, whatever. These are the normal factors in a child's existence. When one or more of them dulls, start looking for the reason.

If you begin to feel your child of any age seems to be having a difficult year, try to find the problem quickly. What exactly is going wrong? Behavior? Peers? Grades? Oppositional behavior toward the teacher? Personality conflict with the teacher or others? There's always a reason. Things don't just happen. Find it. Rough times are inevitable, but if they can be relieved and are not, they become tragic.

Academics will be a serious issue if the child shows ADD tendencies. The non-ADD parent can be a real help if he can spare half an hour a day or so. In that half hour a day, the non-ADD parent can, foremost, figure out how to help the child learn. The parent knows the theory of what makes an ADD child tick. Here's where the parent can somehow put that theory into practice. Can you use buttons from the button box to teach hands-on arithmetic? Dance flash cards across the tabletop because kinesthetic learners respond well to motion? Work things out. Try things.

In that half hour daily, the non-ADD parent can reinforce school work simply by investing the self. "Mommy and Daddy consider this very important. It must be important." If the non-ADD parent can maintain enthusiasm for learning, can brush off frustration when it seems no progress is made, can keep plugging, the child will eventually advance with the strides of giants. It may not seem that way at the time. Trust me. It's so.

School, as important as it is, is not the place where your child will learn the day-to-day skills of living. The ADD parent is the child's primary teacher, as is every other parent. The ADD adult can teach wonderful life skills.

Teaching Day-to-Day Skills

I'm sure that when our kids first came along, Jeri wasn't so certain she wanted me to be teaching them anything at all. She with her left-brain orderliness wasn't about to trust me in my ADD to be able to offer any kind of valuable lessons. She denies this now, of course, but at that time we had not yet really come to realize the source of the differences between us.

What does the ADD parent have to offer, and how does a non-ADD mate fit in? There are many lessons we can impart, by instruction and by example. One of these is a skill we ourselves have to fight constantly to maintain, task completion.

Teach Task Completion

"Do as I say and not as I do" won't cut it. The ADD parent must model this particular struggle for the child. If Mom or Dad can do it, the child sees hope that he can master the skill as well. Besides modeling, the parents should take specific steps in guiding the child toward mastery.

One such step is that the parent, ADD or no, should never lump the child's chores together. You don't ask an ADD child, even an adolescent, to take out the garbage and sweep the porch. You tell the child there are two chores to be done this morning, then ask the child to take out the garbage. That done, you request the sweeping job. For the older child, you tack the two chores up separately on the fridge, asking the child to remove each reminder when the job is done.

One thing at a time. Be very specific. Keep activities separated into small, nonthreatening increments. This is exactly the same approach the ADD adult takes, but you modify it at a child's level for a child's simpler, less mature abilities.

As the child enters her teens, two tasks at a time is not too much to ask. But please don't overwhelm the person with a list or a long lecture, for that matter.

As a second step toward mastering the skill of finishing the job, ask the child to repeat the instructions. This works very well for me. Jeri asks me to do something and I repeat the request back to her. It helps firm the job up in my mind, and it insures that I got the request straight. It will work the same way for your child. Especially as kids get older, this simple act of repeating back requests and instructions bears good fruit. The non-ADD adult may become bored or wearied with constantly getting a playback. To which I say, "hang in there."

A third step is, as soon as the skill is age appropriate, teach list making. The easier it is for ADD-children to get their brains down on paper, the better they will get along. Put big calendars on the inside of the child's door. Hang lists on the fridge. A friend of mine once scotch-taped a note saying FEED ME in big block print on the scruff of the dog's neck. Her daughter was thereby reminded of that particular daily chore.

Fourth, consider helping. If a chore is particularly lengthy or onerous, Jeri will frequently pitch in and help Chip or me. Even if she doesn't do a whole lot, her willingness to work alongside us encourages us greatly. The non-ADD adult might keep that in mind. In a way, it's symbolic; "I'm in this with you." Emblematic or not, it contributes greatly to our oneness as a family.

Finally, monitor progress and make certain the task was indeed completed. Don't evaluate with the scowling eagle eye of the stereotype fault-finder. You're not finding fault. You're keeping the child on the job, teaching responsibility and the discipline of finishing what was started. Responsibility is an important asset to instill.

Again, here the ADD adult must take the lead by example and the non-ADD adult point out the mate's success.

TEACH RESPONSIBILITY

More and more, I've come to appreciate the value of "You." Now our Chip is a night owl. He can howl into the wee hours, but he has a hard time getting up in the morning. So the night before, I'll say something like, "Chip, do *you* want me to get *you* up at seven or at seven-thirty tomorrow?" He tells me what he wants. The next morning, I can say, "Chip? *You* told me to get *you* up now so *you* can watch a little TV before school." Or whatever. The guideline is, Chip has ownership of his own behavior, some control of his life—at least, as much as is appropriate for a kid his age. He is held responsible for his actions and decisions.

Jeri, incidentally, does the same for Chip, and also for me. She's learned to volley the ball into my court and then remind me it's there.

There are different kinds of responsibility, of course. One sort is blame, if you interpret *blame* as being the cause of things both good and bad. Accepting one's personal role in consequences. The other is dependability. Responsibility for a clean room. Responsibility for a broken window. Responsibility for daily tasks—taking out the garbage and making sure the dog is fed.

Teaching responsibility goes hand in hand with teaching and allowing control because control is so heavy in an ADD person's life. Notice when I give Chip control of his life to an appropriate degree, as in the example of asking him what time to get up, the responsibility becomes his. He made the choice; he has to live with it.

Obviously, you can't give a five-year-old the choice of when to go to bed and when to get up. But that child can choose which story will be read. Control options must be appropriate to the child's age. Consider a teen as being close enough to adulthood to accept adult-level responsibility. In fact, sometimes allowing preteens to taste adult responsibility actually improves their motivation and skills.

Sometimes you can invent a few choices for the child to make, just so the child can experience some feeling of being in control. Try to keep it subtle. For example, to promote brushing the teeth before bed, provide the child with two toothbrushes, each fancy, each a different color or design. The child then might choose which of the two to use tonight. Have her choose among two or three breakfast cereals. Let him decide between peas and corn for supper, but make it clear that "neither" is not an acceptable choice.

Sometimes you can offer choices that aren't choices at all; you know perfectly well what the kid will do, but your offering gives him or her the illusion of control. "Hey, [ten-year-old] Chip, want to go along to the hardware store?" Of course he does. "I'm baking cookies. Can you help?" Is she going to say no to an offer like that?

Holding the reins of control not only improves responsibility, it teaches self-worth. "I can choose. My choice is respected. I'm clearly an individual of some weight."

That all ties into self-image, extremely important for any child and especially so for the ADD child.

Teach Self-Worth

What are the tools for enhancing a sense of self-worth? Praise, of course. Kudos. Cheers. Support. Encouragement. That all goes without saying, so I won't say anything.

The non-ADD adult will keep in mind, I hope, that in the big wild world, non-ADD is the goal, the norm, the ideal. Therefore, anything coming from the non-ADD adult is gilded with that luster. Anyone can praise the child. Praise from an admired left brainer (and down inside, even if not on the surface, kids admire their parents) weighs heavily. So does criticism. It bites deep indeed coming from the mouth of someone who, according to the world, has it all together. It's a responsibility the non-ADD parent must keep in mind constantly.

Jeri tells Chip often—several times a day—that she loves him and is proud of him. She doesn't just mouth the pretty words. She tells him why. She claims she can always find a few items of excellence in his day to praise him about. She doesn't have to force a nice word or be patronizing.

Go ahead and patronize a six-year-old. Don't try it with a twelve-year-old, let alone an adult. A "There, there, dear" approach is maddening to the person mature enough to recognize a superior or condescending attitude when she sees it. Worse, that kind of condescension wrecks self-esteem.

So does failure, particularly for the ADD adult or near-adult. Be aware of this caustic side effect of failure and do your best to counteract it with praise, positive comment, and encouragement.

You see, because we impulsively barge right into an idea, action, or project without looking down the road to gauge consequences, we see a high failure rate for our attempts and dreams. Things don't pan out the way we envisioned them, or we lose interest and fail to complete them.

The left brainer, given to analysis anyway, encounters a failure of some sort, figures out why it failed, and avoids that behavior pattern the next time. Not us. We plunge merrily ahead into the next project, again without a clue as to consequences, and get all fouled up again. In short, we do not learn much from failures and mistakes.

Kids and adults both react to failure in several ways. We may adopt an attitude that says, "I failed; therefore I'm no good"—a dandy esteem-wrecker. Or we leap merrily into denial. "It wasn't my fault!" Neither reaction serves any good purpose.

The parent, and in particular the non-ADD parent, must not expect failures and mistakes to be any kind of learning experience. Don't say, "There, you see? I warned you not to loan your camera to a near stranger but you did anyway, and now it's gone. I hope you've learned something from this." Rest assured the ADD child has not. The next time, that person may be just as likely to make the same mistake. And on both occasions the ADD person will either see it as someone else's fault or as evidence of self worthlessness. Neither occasion will serve as a lesson.

Both occasions may trigger anger in the child as well as the parents.

Teach Anger Management by Managing Yours

Whose anger? Yours and your child's. If you are the ADD parent of an ADD child, you will both naturally tend to flare up instantly, and that never improves the situation. And it is so very, very easy to let anger destroy the lesson you are trying to impart. It happens all the time.

Jeri says, "It's so frustrating. Chip will get ten or fifteen good strokes in a row. 'Chip, you did this right.' 'Good job, Chip!' 'Way to go, Chip!' And then we'll correct him on one little thing. What do we get? 'You never praise me! You only criticize!' It's intensely frustrating because it's not true. But Chip really, genuinely believes it's true when he says it. It's as if his anger blinded him to all those previous positive strokes."

It did.

The same thing will happen for you as well. It's not easily correctable. You don't pause and tally good strokes on a wall, so many slash marks a day, in order to show how positive the reinforcement has been. Probably that wouldn't help anyway to convince a child otherwise during the heat of an angry exchange. Reason sometimes doesn't work on ADD people (frankly, reason doesn't work well on non-ADD people at times, either, but that's beside the point).

Be prepared for it. Don't be surprised when it comes.

Anger is a poor time for anything, not just recalling positive reinforcement. In our house we try never to debate issues when tensions run high. It's not a good course of action with non-ADD adults, and it's an even worse course of action with ADD people. Without the usual restraints on behavior or the ability to smolder, we blow up immediately and say just about anything. The ADD parent blowing and the ADD child blowing are like two volcanoes trying to out-puff each other. What's the point?

There are lines to be drawn. The child must know there is never any excuse for violence. Never, particularly in the home. This again is something the child learns best by osmosis from the parents. If Mom and Dad keep hands off each other, statistically the child's not likely to be a batterer.

The arguments for and against martial arts training are prolific, and I won't go into all of them here. Some parents feel that training an ADD child or teen in bare-handed martial skills gives that person a self-discipline and self-confidence nothing else can. Further, the training minimizes the possibility of harm during and after school. (It's sad that life has come to that. Kids aren't safe in the halls anymore, and certainly not outside the school's cyclone fence.) Others feel that because an ADD kid has such a hair-trigger, likely to boil over in fury too quickly to think, martial arts training is dangerous for everyone else around.

In making a decision about self-protection or martial arts training for your child, weigh the child's nature carefully. You know him best. What does this particular child—forget about the millions of other kids—need? What are your convictions regarding the subject? You want to violate neither your personal beliefs nor the child's needs.

In any case, no matter how much stress the ADD child's or adult's learning differences cause, the person must learn not to abuse, to injure, to overreact. The non-ADD family member may well be the one to remind others of this.

Remember too the golden rule of ADD argument: When one person's voice starts to rise, the other's voice goes down. Even small children can understand that principle. In fact, a small child with no defenses against the huge, angry adult, will welcome that rule.

Jeri and I are very careful when correcting Chip to maintain a pleasant, conversational, level tone of voice. Anger begets anger instantly in an ADD person. Chip handles life pretty good-naturedly unless we get in his face. Then he torches instantly. So no matter what the situation, we try to keep anger out of it.

Especially when they're small, ADD children who erupt in fury are accused of showing off, of creating a scene for personal attention. Now I'm the first to admit that that can be the case. But most outbursts of anger are genuine, even if they serve an ulterior purpose. So while in a sense the kid is guilty as charged, it's not as if the child or teen can deliberately abstain from angry outbursts. The trick is to learn to minimize them. Part of that trick lies in minimizing the attention they bring.

When an ADD person, child or adult, erupts, if possible

remove that person from the scene immediately. As soon as cooling off commences, extra one-on-one time with the person should bring home a couple of lessons: 1) acting that way gets you nothing, and 2) I'm there for you anyway.

Remembering that the ADD person needs what every other human being needs, only more of it, one-on-one time with the child or teen is a must. A personal relationship, providing reassurance, guidance, and an anchor in life are the things the adult—especially the non-ADD adult—can bring to the person out of control.

If I were you, I wouldn't bother offering advice or insight when the person is in a reactionary mood—that is, immersed in post-anger grumpiness and defiance. The person is simply not receptive, and your wisdom will slide right off. Teflon. Non-stick. Wait until the grumpiness passes and bring the subject up in a nonthreatening way. "Hey, Chip, remember when you blew up an hour ago? I want to talk about that."

Chip's reaction might well be, "Huh?" He's already forgotten about it. The ADD adult may have forgotten it as well. That means the non-ADD parent may have to keep plugging, to emphasize truths over and over.

Teach Persistence by Being Persistent

To quote another famous ADD adult, "Never give up. Never give up. Never give up."

Perseverance pays off eventually. The ADD person's two-steps-forward-one-step-back isn't really a 2–1 ratio. It's not that progressive. Sometimes it seems we're not moving forward at all, particularly as an ADD child grows into adolescence and beyond without seeming to be able to remember more than one thing in a row, complete a task, or stay with an assignment. The child grows but the school grades don't rise.

Because the ADD child is such a late bloomer, refrain from giving in. By all means, hang in there! I was in my thirties before I mastered some fairly elementary life skills. I don't think that's atypical for an ADD adult.

This persistence is nice to talk about long range, but it takes its form in daily slogging.

"I told you a dozen times not to do that!"

"Aren't you listening? I asked you to get ready for bed."

"You were warned not to stay out past dark and you did anyway. You don't listen."

Can't this kid remember anything from moment to moment?

The lessons your child would learn must be repeated over and over and over. What seems to have sunk in today will have floated back to the surface tomorrow. Your non-ADD mate in particular will be repeatedly frustrated. Perhaps both of you will start thinking the child is being deliberately lax or forgetful; it's so easy to put the blame on the child, even when down inside you know better.

It's true that sometimes the child doesn't bother trying to remember certain rules and guidelines, particularly when it suits the child not to. *Any* child is like that to an extent. There are dogs that take a cavalier attitude toward the living room rug, too.

So post the basic rules on a closet door or in the laundry room. Spell everything out and revise them often enough that they grow with your child. Rules relax and change as a child grows. What used to be "Never ever cross the street" becomes, eventually, "Look both ways first" and will remain that through life.

Here is a solid line, in black and white. The child may not remember to observe a rule, but he or she knows it's there. That's immensely useful to an ADD person. We don't do well at guessing meets and bounds of a diffusely stated rule or concept. We're not good at what the computer gurus call "fuzzy logic." Also, we do better at following things that are stored somewhere besides just in our head. We consult lists. We consult posted rules. And by that means we remember externally that which simply cannot be dragged up at will internally.

Posted rules teach a secondary lesson that is not to be sneezed

196 Rick and Jerilyn Fowler

at; respect for and understanding of the law. Our rights and limitations are based on a written code. So are the child's.

In all this you see an underlying concept—working with the ADD problem rather than trying to shoehorn the ADD child or adult into a world that will not fit. All this comes across to your child, ideally, as lessons in respect for ADD.

TEACH WHOLENESS AND A RESPECT FOR ADD

In 1 Corinthians 12, Paul promises that God will elevate the handicapped person so that there will be no division in body. The noble and the base will be evened out. Whether the right brainer is noble or base is moot. Whether ADD can qualify as a handicap is moot. The fact remains that God honors the ADD condition just as much as any other.

The ADD adult must make peace with that precept before he or she can hope to impart peace to the child. So must the non-ADD mate; in some regards even more so. Something that affecting and profound is next to impossible to adopt through teaching or conversation. It must be lived.

Some grieving is appropriate, especially as the child approaches adulthood. ADD imparts advantages, but it also causes pain and disadvantage. That pain and hassle, plus the losses they cause, must be grieved just like any other loss or deficit.

But the ADD child and adult more than most people have the gift of being able to put the past behind and move ahead. Grieve, yes. Shake a fist at God, if you must. Then develop an action plan to deal with it from this day on. To build that plan, apply the precepts in this book to daily living. They work to a limited extent for the child. They work much better for the adult that child will soon become.

It's so easy to make doom and gloom predictions. Grass won't grow in sand. Everyone knows that. I can tell you from my own experience, from Jeri's and Chip's, and from that of many of my clients: the highest hurdle is the one inside your head.

You and your child have talents. Let the non-ADD mate

encourage you and aid you along the way. Don't let the non-ADD spouse disparage you; it's easy to do that when two people are so very close. Don't let the world get the best of you for being different. One way or another, use those talents you possess.

If only the best birds sang, the woods would be silent.

THE SUM OF IT ALL

Eventually, your child will come to appreciate more than condemn the condition we've labelled Attention Deficit Disorder. It took me a long, long time. In fact, I'm still in the process. ADD is a powerful, powerful shaping influence in my life—always was, always will be.

The non-ADD mate at times does not appreciate just how overreaching the ADD condition is. The non-ADD mate did not grow up with the criticism—did not live it. Of all the things a non-ADD parent can do that would help, the greatest by far is simply to try to understand. As Jeri will attest, it is incredibly hard to do.

Like errant magi, the suite of differences called ADD brings both gifts and problems. The magi no doubt mean well, but they haven't quite got their act together. Consider the original magi. Gold, frankincense, and myrrh. Myrrh. Embalming spices for a baby boy? I can see the gold, and even the frankincense, but why did they bring the myrrh?

I'd like to reflect on some of the aspects of ADD we haven't looked at much as yet, more for the sake of a non-ADD spouse than for the ADD mate. The ADD mate is at least marginally aware of these various gifts, but the non-ADD spouse may not be. In this book, we've seen to some extent how to circumvent the problems ADD can cause. What about the gifts that the magi bring?

ADDenda: Final Considerations

Jeri speaks:

It's been a long time coming. Rick and I are finally a partnership. When I say our marriage is a partnership, that doesn't mean we walk through life like Tweedledum and Tweedledee, looking alike, talking alike, thinking alike, and wearing pots on our heads for helmets. We're as *un*-alike as you can get. But we work together in harness well. We have balanced and merged our different gifts.

For a while, I thought my life would be ruined, tied until death to a hyperactive man with the attention span of a butterfly and the sensitivity of kudzu. The frustrations blinded me to the blessings. I guess that happens with everyone to some extent. Anyway, the changes in both of us have allowed me to realize how richly I am blessed.

Perhaps this end-of-the-story can encapsulate the changes: Remember I mentioned in the discussion about money that Rick talked me into selling the diamonds in my wedding band so that we could buy a boat? It was a story typical of his impulsivity and his inability to consider consequences. I came to regret that bit of impulsivity, but I didn't say much about it. What's done is done.

On our anniversary some years later, after we both had grown, he replaced the diamonds.

Rick speaks:

I'm almost never calm and collected. I live with constant tension because I can barely control my impulsive behavior. Sometimes I fail in that. Everything seems to be happening all at once around me. I hear only parts of conversations and catch only snatches of information I'm supposed to be absorbing. People think all I care about is myself and that I'm egocentric. I'm constantly griping at myself about my bad habits, a desire for procrastination being one of the worst. I so often feel I can't do anything right, especially when one of my "props" collapses. I'll fail to connect with Jeri oftener than I'll achieve good communication, and that shortfall pains me. I can't naturally get a solid hold on life, or on time, or on my responsibilities.

I have a wonderful life!

I'm not kidding; I really do. All that long paragraph above is the down side. It's not the most important side because the up side by far outweighs it. In addition, my victory comes by *not* yielding to the down side, the low self-esteem and all.

I'm nothing like Jeri, of course, and Jeri possesses splendid qualities which I do not. Through the long process of working things out together, we've come to rely upon each other's gifts. She provides the anchor; I provide the sails. She offers advantages, but so do I.

The Gifts of the Magi

What are the advantages of being an ADD adult? Let me count some ways.

Channelled Correctly, ADD Gets You Places Faster

The magi's gift can be just plain gold. Once we master study methods, which usually work well in any other line of learning endeavor also, we ADD adults have the prerequisites for success in hand. We are usually ambitious, ready to prove ourselves and overcome the "I am dirt" mentality the world has shoehorned us into, and restless to do things.

We're spectacularly successful at jobs which take us on the road, occupations that send us out to meet people. Benjamin Franklin is often cited as the best diplomat who ever served our country. He exhibited quite a few signs of ADD. We're the ones to call when you have to negotiate a tricky agreement or defuse a tense situation. We're endlessly creative in finding solutions, and we can talk your socks off. We can schmooze with the best of them.

The ADD adult who would absolutely bomb out as a bookkeeper or banker can shine as a restaurateur or salesman. The *Time* magazine cover story on ADD adults (in the July 18, 1994 issue) mentions as an example a doctor, Bruce Roseman, with eleven offices in four states. He thrives on an eighteen-hour day, thanks to his ADD. His hyperactivity translates directly into profitable productivity.

Similarly, our impulsivity translates into decisiveness, and that is often lined with gold also. In jobs where quick decisions are required, with no waffling—fire fighting, for example—we're the best. When David Farragut, the Union's brilliant naval officer during the Civil War, was warned of enemy torpedoes as he entered Mobile Bay, he ignored the warning and roared, "Full steam ahead!" That's pure ADD! However, we're not totally reckless. Some naval historians believe Farragut had already received intelligence from ashore that the Confederate torpedoes had been disabled.

Still, we're comfortable taking chances. We can leave behind the secure job and step out into new arenas, and we don't often mope. It helps in the workaday world to be able to put grudges behind, and we do. Also, we are good at seizing the moment.

Our non-ADD mate, usually a more cautious person, reticent about stepping out blindly, can put the brakes on us. But I caution that non-ADD spouse against too much braking. Certainly it may be to your dual advantage to temper hasty plans and action. But tempering is not the same as stopping. Let us fly, and we will bring you with us.

ADD Allows You an Exciting Career Life

With degrees in psychology and education, I am prepared for any of several careers. I've succeeded in more than one, and I'm not all that old. The ADD adult is always looking ahead to interesting new prospects. Few aging ADD adults have to look back with regret to opportunities not seized and avenues not explored. We can't do it all, but we sure try. Best of all, we can make a real and positive difference in other people's lives. Now there is a lovely and rewarding gift the magi have bestowed.

The non-ADD mate may not understand that we crave changes and are prepared to make them. The non-ADD spouse may use phrases like "put up with his restlessness," or sentences such as, "She has a good career. Why does she want to change?" Please support us. We'll do better in the long run if we cater to our need for change.

And what about that great thief of happiness, boredom? Not a problem.

ADD Adults Are Hardly Ever Bored

Frankincense. Sweetly aromatic, symbolic of the spirit. The magi bring a gift of spiritedness, which is what the word *enthusiasm* means. The more I talk to worried, disgruntled people, the happier I am that I have this innate desire to constantly get out and do new things. Flying—what a blast! Fixing an old beater car or motorcycle up into something that turns heads as you drive down the street. Taking Jeri and the kids out to great places to do fun things. Travel. I love it all! ADD adults tend to maintain their enthusiasm throughout life.

Even better, we impart that excitement to our spouses. Jeri claims that her life is never boring and she loves it that way. That delights me beyond words! How many spouses hunger to bring pleasure to the people they love, only to find boredom or drudgery prevailing instead? The magi gave me a gift to share, and I am much the richer for sharing.

Do you know one of the saddest first lines I ever came across in a book? It's from the original novel *Quo Vadis,* by Henryk Sienkiewicz. The line is, "Petronius woke only about midday, and as usual greatly wearied." Those pitiful words describe so very many people.

Life, my friends, is not a dress rehearsal.

Best of all, the ADD's relationship with God through Jesus can be deliciously vivid. Frankincense, the gift of a sweet aroma toward God, is another of the magi's gifts to us.

Our Spiritual Walk Can Be Very Satisfying

There is an unusual degree of guilt in an ADD Christian's life. Trust me on that. For example, it's corporate prayer time. Our group is getting heavily into meaningful and powerful prayer. Lives are changing or about to be changed. Everyone is sweating with effort. Except me. A couple minutes into a prayer session, my mind tends to wander. Do I feel guilty about that or what?

Liturgy and repetitious activity bore me in a hurry. I'm supposed to be praising and worshiping God, and instead I'm wishing this part of the service or that were over with.

That's the negative part.

The positive part is that I feel a special oneness with Jesus, and that in itself outweighs a lot of negative aspects. Like ADD adults, He spoke His mind without regard to whom He irritated. Listen to Him castigate the Pharisees with His "Woe unto you!" for instance. He felt about hypocrisy the same as I feel about hypocrisy. That's pure right-brain stuff! He had Scripture memorized, down pat, and He could present a linear argument better than any scholar He ever encountered—perfectly left-brained. He was perfectly both-brained, obviously, the Savior for all people—the likes of Peter and Paul, a host of dedicated believers throughout the ages, my beloved Jeri, and me.

He forgives my sins and shortcomings. That is immensely liberating to me because ADD adults more than many are constantly made aware of their shortcomings. He heals my great vat of guilt with His ocean of love and forgiveness. I am very personally grateful to Him. He promised that He came to give us life abundantly, and I do indeed enjoy an abundant life.

Every human being is a sinner, and every human being needs Jesus Christ, but the ADD adult can perhaps understand that easier. The left brainer is praised by men and feels a certain superiority. The left brainer is usually on top of things, in nominal control of life. The left brainer, therefore, doesn't always recognize that every person, the overachiever included, is a poor, out-of-control, wretched, needy sinner in God's eyes.

Oh, but we ADD adults—we've been told all our lives how far short we fall. Our only problem is receiving freely the most gracious gift of God Himself, acceptance into His family of perfect people. We're not used to being perfect, even if our perfection is bestowed upon us from outside. What a joy it is when we understand the gospel!

Our Weakness Is Our Strength

Of the gifts of the magi, myrrh is perhaps the most curious. The Hebrews as well as the Egyptians used the strange odor of myrrh in worship and in the preparation of bodies for burial.

Gathered from scraggly bushes, myrrh is a gum with a nasty, haunting taste and aroma. You can't eat it. Too bitter. Used as incense, it is what we might call an acquired taste. Pretty odorous. It's not sweet or beautiful. And yet true myrrh is extremely valuable, in demand, and hard to find. What myrrh does it does well.

To many people, ADD adults are hard to live with, annoying,

difficult to work beside, impossible to understand well. To them, we're an acquired taste—not sweet like frankincense or beautiful like gold. But what we can do we do very well. We provide unique gifts the world can use and we receive unique gifts, as from those inscrutable magi.

You and your spouse possess unique gifts which you can offer God and the world, gifts of gold, frankincense, and myrrh.

I adjure you to enjoy them and use them well, together.

JERI'S STORY

During the first five years of my marriage to Rick Fowler, I lived in four states in six different houses. Some people wouldn't blink an eye. Rick didn't. But I was a small-town girl who grew up in one place. Until Rick, I had moved only once in my life—ten miles from one small burg to another. As I contemplated still another move, I got to thinking about all the other unusual or just plain irritating things about my husband. Maybe Dad was right. Maybe this marriage had been a dreadful mistake.

When we married between our sophomore and junior years of college, both sets of parents moaned that we were acting too impulsively and privately feared it would never last. I was much too quiet for him. He was much too impulsive and unstable for me. He had a dark side, able to become furious instantly. He bounced around like a Kewpie doll on a rubber string. I heard all sorts of arguments.

Rick might go ballistic over some small inconvenience or

injustice way out of proportion to its importance. His explosive anger frightened me. Though he never ever hurt me physically, he was expert at cutting me with sharp words. Hours after he'd ruined my day, or my week, or my life, he'd be all cuddly and cheerful, as if nothing had happened. I could have strangled him.

And his projects! Not only did he try to carve out five or six careers, he always had these "great" (his assessment) projects. We went through so many cars, boats, and motorcycles, I lost count. He'd buy a beater, fix it up, and sell it. Sometimes he wouldn't even fix it up. He should have been a junk dealer. His enthusiasm, often as not, sort of sucked me up into the project with him. I've already told you about the time he talked me into selling the diamonds out of my wedding band so that we could buy a boat we'd both had our eye on. He was that kind of pied piper.

Oh, he had his brilliance. I tended to give in to fate. If I got a traffic ticket, I got a traffic ticket. *Que sera sera.* No *sera* for Rick. When he got a citation he thought was unjust, he took it to court, representing himself, and won. He was twenty-two. I admired his guts and his pizzazz!

But.

He hated reading for pleasure. I grew up in a highly literate atmosphere where reading was tantamount to happiness. His lack of interest in books disturbed me. He didn't like Scrabble or Trivial Pursuit or Boggle—the kind of intellectually stimulating games I thrived on.

But my greatest sadness was his attitude toward family. Over and over, he insisted he could never settle down and be a father. As far as he was concerned, living in one place and raising kids was a millstone he would never chain around his neck. He was adamant about that, and it tore me apart. I have six brothers and sisters. I'm family-oriented. I'd always anticipated having a big, wonderful family like my parents did. Here I was married to a gypsy with no redeeming family characteristics.

Time didn't improve anything. Things that I used to shrug

off with, "That's just Rick" during the first bloom of our romance were beginning to deeply embarrass me. The charming
spontaneity and unconventional attitudes that had first drawn
me to him were fast souring. He badmouthed holiday traditions
and went out of his way to avoid being associated with them.
Worse, this guy said whatever he thought. If it came to his mind,
who knows from where, it popped out his mouth instantly. That
which I used to call "impulsive" was fast becoming "repulsive."
How could I ever have fallen in love with this madman?

When did it turn around? I'm not sure. The first change was
in me, I believe.

I remember an occasion when our church featured a highly
touted guest speaker, a man in the upper brackets of our denom-
inational structure. His presentation was elegant, suave, and
utterly devoid of instruction or encouragement. In clusters after
the service, our friends muttered about how little they had received from his message. Yet one by one, they shook the
speaker's hand and told him how much they enjoyed his talk.

I tried to mumble something polite and slip past, but Rick
smiled, took the speaker's hand, and said quite sincerely, "Sir,
I'd like you to know that was one of the worst sermons I've ever
heard."

I almost melted into the floor, a little puddle at the speaker's
shoes.

And yet, Rick had the courage to speak as Jesus Himself
would have spoken, calling a spade a spade. What if the church
did more of that, pure honesty and less hypocrisy?

No hypocrite, Rick. He never once wavered from the man-
dates of Scripture as he saw them, though, of course, his vision
of God's Word has matured with time. For someone with such
a cavalier attitude toward life and authority, he was extremely
rigid about matters of theology and faith.

That was what held us together during those early years. I
promised my father I would never divorce, and Rick was as
determined as I to remain true to our marriage bond. I'm certain
that without Jesus we would have lost each other.

Rick's ways perplexed me. They mystified me. And then I learned that Rick was just as perplexed and mystified about himself as was I.

Along came Chip. As he approached kindergarten, he began to display the same kind of impulsive, active, living-on-the-edge personality his father had. If I had to live with two men like that, I thought, I'd go nuts! But as we dealt with Chip's emerging problems, we began to gain insight into Rick's life. In the light of Chip's ADD, Rick's undiagnosed "peculiarities" suddenly made sense.

Now at last I was beginning to realize that all those pesky habits and tendencies that I used to see as Rick's shortcomings were neither deliberate nor preventable. He was doing the best he could. Encouraged, I took greater pains to adjust—to move together in harness with him better. I tried to be more affirmative and positive, to praise more.

Both Chip and Rick have changed immensely in these last years. So have I. And it has made all the difference.

RICK'S STORY

I didn't find out I was dumb until the fourth grade. That's when the chip on my shoulder started to grow.

You see, I'm a missionary's kid, so kindergarten through third grade I spent in a mission compound in Guatemala, where my mom home-schooled me using the Calvert system, which is used a lot by missionaries overseas. In that less structured atmosphere, one on one with someone with patience who knew me well, I did just fine. Then we returned to the States, I entered a formal school, and my world took a nosedive.

My fourth-grade teacher sent my report card home with comments like, "Rick is a nice boy, but he has trouble staying focused." "He can't seem to stay at his desk." "His mind wanders a lot." In the classroom atmosphere, I simply could not stick to work. Everyone else could. I got poor grades. Nearly everyone else got better ones. Obviously, it was me. My self-image started a downhill slide that just kept going into high school, dragging my grades with it.

And then I discovered basketball.

My older brothers were good at the game, and they didn't play "nice" ball, not toward little brother Ricky. I learned elbow-ball from the best.

In high school I was usually a starter and racked up an average of thirty-one points per game. Sure, I was popular. Sure, I enjoyed the respect and heady success that athletics offer. But if I was such a hotshot, why couldn't I score academically? How come everyone else could pass tests comfortably except me? The chip on my shoulder became a granite block, and I developed a reputation for aggressive play bordering on hostility. My points-per-game average probably would have been higher if I hadn't fouled out so much.

In our family the rule was, "Fight and you're grounded." So I learned quickly enough never to throw a punch. Physically. Boy, could I lay it on verbally! I became the master of the nasty cut. Acid tongue. Flame thrower. There's where my aggression really blossomed.

Proving others wrong, especially those who carried authority, did a lot for me, so to speak. It propped up my flagging self-image—"If I'm right and you're wrong, I'm better." It got me to heights I never would have achieved otherwise, and it just about destroyed me. That's a lot to expect from any personality quirk.

For example, I wanted so badly to prove my high school guidance counselor wrong when he said, "Don't even think about college," that I signed up for college. My junior year, I took a philosophy course that was the dread of all those A and B students, brains who were pleased to be able to pull a C. That philosophy course . . .

After we had turned in two papers, the professor called me into his office to, he said, "review your work." Here it came again; like my old guidance counselor, he was going to tell me to get out of academics. Instead, he handed me back my two papers—with high marks!

"Your writing skills are rudimentary," he complained. "But allowing for that, when I look past the inability to express yourself well, I see one of the sharper minds I've ever encountered."

Sharp? Old 2.2 GPA Fowler?

That interview changed my whole outlook on life. Certainly, it was God's doing, His instrument for turning me around. Probably, I was softened up, so to speak, and ready to turn around. And turn around I did. That renewed confidence in my mental acuity fired me up so that I never made less than a B from then on. Eventually I would complete a master's degree, a specialist degree, an Ed.D. and the requirements for a licensed counselor.

I was too obtuse, however, to see the torment I was putting Jeri through. She tried to shrug off the caustic responses with which I blasted her every time I got excited or angry. She tried to resist being annoyed with my impulsivity and perpetual motion. She was open. She certainly was no stick-in-the-mud with a built-in dour frown. But she wasn't happy, either.

As I began to gain genuine control in some areas of my life, such as academics, I started looking at other areas. And the treatment of my wife was one of the most discomforting parts of my behavior. Now I have long been sensitive to what God expects as expressed in Scripture. Sometimes, early in my life as a Christian, my interpretation was a little off-base or immature—not in matters of faith so much as in matters of practice. Everyone grows in that regard. I did. Here was God's Word telling me to honor my wife, respect her, be gracious toward her (toward everybody; not just Jeri!), gladden her heart. And then there was the matter of children. God's Word valued them highly; I was avoiding them.

I began applying Scripture's lessons and principles about getting along with family, about marriage, that I so glibly taught everyone else. I've learned to self-talk myself out of disabling patterns of thought into more productive ones. I've learned that even if I'm not sensitive to Jeri's needs and feelings, I must allow her to show me what I'm not seeing. I've learned most of all to curb my acid tongue and sarcastic attitude—to bite off that nasty word before it gets out of my mouth.

I'm not proud of the old Rick Fowler. Although the new Rick Fowler is an improvement, he's not there yet. But I have hope. I never used to.

God taught me a lot about the needs and beauties of family, once I was receptive to His lessons. It hasn't come easily. By the measures the world applies, Jeri had every right to give up the fight and leave me to stew in my own caustic juices. She's hung in. I've hung in.

The best is yet to come!

ADD Quiz

Me Mate

__ __   1. I have trouble sitting quietly for an extended length of time. I need to be on the move.

__ __   2. It's easy for me to lose interest in games, books, work, or conversations.

__ __   3. Sometimes people get upset with me and I have no idea why.

__ __   4. I hate schedules and routines. I want to eat when I'm hungry and sleep when I'm tired.

__ __   5. I usually have several projects going at once. I thrive on constant variety.

_✓_ _—_   6. I remember faces but tend to forget names.

_✓_ _—_   7. I can follow people who have my respect, but I don't like to submit to people just because they're in a position of authority.

_✓_ _—_   8. When I get really excited about something, I can't sit still and stay focused.

_✓_ _—_   9. I easily get the big picture, but I don't care much about details.

_—_ _—_   10. I believe in saying what you think, without worrying much about what is socially "nice."

_—_ _—_   11. "Relax" means shifting gears and doing something else, not stalling into neutral.

_✓_ _—_   12. I get more done sprawled in a chair or sitting on the floor than I can at a desk.

_✓_ _—_   13. I'll forget things that will be important later; going out the door without my coat or keys, for instance.

_—_ _—_   14. I'll forget, or consider trivial, things that my mate considers important. Grocery stops, for example.

_✓_ _—_   15. I've been accused of interrupting too much and asking too many questions.

_✓_ _—_   16. People say I'm too inconsistent. I think they're overstating it.

_ _ 17. Risks are where it's at. They make life vivid.

✓ _ 18. Action around me or other thoughts frequently draw me away from the task at hand.

✓ _ 19. Some say my desk or work area is usually a mess. I can generally find what I need there.

_ _ 20. When something cries out to be done, you do it, and you worry about consequences later.

Five or fewer checks suggest that ADD and extreme right-brain orientation are not significant factors in your life. More than five suggest an impulsive personality, possibly with the presence of some ADD signs and symptoms. If either partner scores eleven or more checks, impulsivity is probably causing problems in your marriage right now.

If that is the case, the health of your marriage requires that each of you makes some changes. We hope this book is a help and a blessing to you.

About the Authors

Dr. Rick Fowler is director of Outpatient Services at the Minirth Meier New Life Clinic in Richardson, Texas. He holds a doctoral degree in the field of social psychology.

Over the past twenty-four years, Dr. Fowler has served at three colleges as a professor of psychology, head basketball coach, and athletic director. He has acted as a consultant and management trainer for a wide variety of corporations and groups and has been a consultant to several professional sports teams. He has over eighteen years of counseling experience and is a licensed professional counselor and marriage and family therapist.

Dr. Fowler has conducted numerous seminars for various groups and industries across North America and throughout the world. He has published numerous articles in national periodicals and has authored nine books. He is a frequent guest on the Minirth Meier New Life Clinic radio program and represents the clinic as a speaker and teacher on a national level.

Jerilyn Fowler holds a master's degree in English Education from the University of Georgia. She taught on the college and high school levels before starting a family. In addition, she has been a freelance writer and editor and Bible study teacher for the past fifteen years.

Rick and Jeri have been married more than twenty-six years and have two children—a daughter, Jodi, and a son, Chip.